LUCENT LIBRARY *of* HISTORICAL ERAS

MUMMIES, MYTH, AND MAGIC:
RELIGION IN ANCIENT EGYPT

DON NARDO

LUCENT BOOKS

An imprint of Thomson Gale, a part of The Thomson Corporation

THOMSON

GALE

Detroit • New York • San Francisco • San Diego • New Haven, Conn. • Waterville, Maine • London • Munich

THOMSON

---✦---

GALE

© 2005 Thomson Gale, a part of The Thomson Corporation.

Thomson and Star Logo are trademarks and Gale and Lucent Books are registered trademarks used herein under license.

For more information, contact
Lucent Books
27500 Drake Rd.
Farmington Hills, MI 48331-3535
Or you can visit our Internet site at http://www.gale.com

LIBRARY OF CONGRESS CATALOGING-IN-PUBLICATION DATA

Nardo, Don, 1947–
    Mummies, myth, and magic : religion in ancient Egypt / by Don Nardo.
      p. cm. — (The Lucent library of historical eras)
Includes bibliographical references and (p.   ) and index.
ISBN 1-59018-707-5 (hardcover : alk. paper)
1. Egypt—Religion. I. Title. II. Series.
BL2441.3.N37 2005
299'.31—dc22
                                                  2005008135

Printed in the United States of America

Contents

Foreword   4

Introduction
The World's Most Religious People?   6

Chapter One
The Gods and Their Realm   10

Chapter Two
Major Creation Myths   22

Chapter Three
Rituals to Honor the Gods   30

Chapter Four
Magic Spells and Amulets   40

Chapter Five
Beliefs About the Afterlife   49

Chapter Six
Mummies and Embalming   58

Chapter Seven
Rituals to Honor the Dead   66

Chapter Eight
Tombs and Grave Goods   75

Chapter Nine
Tomb Robbers Violate the Dead   84

Epilogue
The Legacy of Egyptian Religion   93

Notes   96
Chronology   99
Glossary   100
For Further Reading   102
Works Consulted   104
Index   107
Picture Credits   112
About the Author   112

Foreword

Looking back from the vantage point of the present, history can be viewed as a myriad of intertwining roads paved by human events. Some paths stand out—broad highways whose mileposts, even from a distance of centuries, are clear. The events that propelled the rise to power of Germany's Third Reich, its role in World War II, and its eventual demise, for example, are well defined and documented.

Other roads are less distinct, their route sometimes hidden from view. Modern legislatures may have developed from old tribal councils, for example, but the links between them are indistinct in places, open to discussion and interpretation.

The architecture of civilization—law, religion, art, science, and government—as well as the more everyday aspects of our culture—what we eat, what we wear—all developed along the historical roads and byways. In that progression can be traced every facet of modern life.

A broad look back along these roads reveals that many paths—though of vastly different character—seem to converge at a few critical junctions. These intersections are those great historical eras that echo over the long, steady course of human history, extending beyond the past and into the present.

These epic periods of time are the focus of Lucent's Library of Historical Eras. They shine through the mists of history like beacons, illuminated by a burst of creativity that propels events forward—so bright that we, from thousands of years away, can clearly see the chain of events leading to the present.

Each Lucent Library of Historical Eras consists of a set of books that highlight various aspects of these major eras. For example, the Elizabethan England library features volumes on Queen Elizabeth I and her court, Elizabethan theater, the great playwrights, and everyday life in Elizabethan London.

The mini-library approach allows for the division of each era into its most significant and most interesting parts and the exploration of those parts in depth. Also, social and cultural trends as well as illustrative documents and eyewitness accounts can be prominently featured in individual volumes.

Lucent's Library of Historical Eras presents a wealth of information to young readers. The lively narrative, fully documented primary and secondary source quotations, maps, photographs, sidebars, and annotated bibliographies serve as launching points for class discussion and further research.

In studying the great historical eras, students also develop a better understanding of our own times. What we learn from the past and how we apply it in the present may shape the future and may determine whether our era will be a guiding light to those traveling future roads.

Introduction

THE WORLD'S MOST RELIGIOUS PEOPLE?

When historians write about the cultures and lives of ancient peoples, they almost invariably include descriptions of the gods and the religious beliefs and practices of these peoples. This is understandable. The vast majority of Greeks, Romans, Babylonians, Persians, Etruscans, Celts, and other inhabitants of the ancient Mediterranean-European sphere were deeply religious. In fact, faith in and the worship and appeasement of divine forces played a bigger role in their lives than it does in the lives of most people today.

However, even the peoples mentioned above were not as culturally immersed in religious ideas and activities as the ancient Egyptians were. And travelers from neighboring lands readily acknowledged this fact. In the fifth century B.C., the Greek historian Herodotus paid an extended visit to Egypt and was struck by the level of faith and piety he observed among the populace. "They are religious to excess, beyond any other nation in the world," he said of the natives. Herodotus even went so far as to theorize that many Greek gods and religious practices originated in Egypt. "In ancient times," he said,

the Pelasgians [early inhabitants of Greece] offered sacrifices of all kinds, and prayed to the gods, but without any distinction of name or title, for they had not yet heard of any such thing. . . . The names of the gods were brought into Greece from Egypt and the Pelasgians learned them. . . . [For] it was only—if I may so put it—the day before yesterday that the Greeks came to know the origin and form of the various gods, and whether or not all of them had always existed.[1]

Herodotus likely exaggerated the religious links between early Egypt and early Greece. However, he did not exaggerate the high degree of sincere piety among Egyptians of all walks of life. One of the leading classical scholars of the twentieth century, the late Lionel Casson, summed it up this way:

> Religion permeated an Egyptian's total existence. In his eyes, every detail of his own life, and of the life about him . . . was a specific, calculated act of a god. [These included everything from] the annual inundation of the Nile [a yearly flood in which the river's level gently rose and irrigated nearby fields] . . . [to] the chance death of [a] cat. We of the West can place religion in a compartment of its own. We can say, "Render unto Caesar the things that are Caesar's and to God the things that are God's," but not an Egyptian. His Caesar was the pharaoh [ruler], and the pharaoh was a god. . . . Even in [ancient Egyptian] politics the [all-encompassing] presence of religion is clear. The great administrative officials at the pharaoh's court were at the same time prelates [high priests] of the church.[2]

Efforts to Harness Natural Forces

The Egyptians believed that natural events and cycles such as the Nile's flooding were divine acts. This belief highlights a crucial

This painting from the early New Kingdom shows the importance the ancient Egyptians placed on cattle. Several of their gods were depicted in bovine form.

Chapter One

The Gods and Their Realm

The ancient Egyptians worshipped hundreds of gods, and their concept of divine beings was both wide ranging and complex. This is especially true when Egyptian religion is compared with more modern monotheistic religions such as Judaism, Christianity, and Islam, which feature the much simpler concept of a single, all-powerful god. The Egyptians' more diverse and complex religious vision is reflected in their general word for "god"—*netcher*. *Netcher* could refer to a great and powerful deity such as Osiris, lord of the Underworld, or it could refer to Amun-Ra, the chief god of the New Kingdom (the period lasting from 1550 to 1069 B.C., when the Egyptian realm reached its height of power and influence). The term could also be used to describe various minor deities with limited powers, such as Mehen, a serpent god who protected the sun god.

The word *netcher* also generally denoted dangerous or harmful supernatural beings, such as demons. In addition, it could refer to humans, usually kings, who had been deified (given the status of a god) or to ordinary dead people who returned to earth as ghosts. In turn, more specific terms were often used to describe some of these beings, who were widely feared. According to Richard Wilkinson:

> Even the earliest religious writings [of ancient Egypt] are peopled with frightening creatures (especially Underworld monsters and demon-like beings). . . . The ghosts or spirits of the deceased were also feared by the Egyptians and were known as *akhu*. . . . But the most commonly feared beings were the messengers and *bau* of deities. *Bau* were manifestations [alternate forms] . . . of a god [or gods, who] sent their *bau* to punish or trouble the [human] offender.[7]

General Categories of Gods

To help sort through the huge and potentially confusing assemblage of Egyptian gods and spirits, some modern experts have attempted to divide them into various categories. There is evidence to suggest that the Egyptians themselves sometimes placed their deities in such general groups, although the practice, along with the nature of these groups, remains unclear and probably varied widely from place to place.

One important way to differentiate among the gods seems to have been to view some as major, national deities and others as minor, local ones. The now familiar, highly developed religious system in place in Egypt from roughly 3100 to 100 B.C. was assembled from numerous, more ancient localized cults (modes or systems of belief and worship). So a mix of national and local gods remained a central feature of Egyptian religion. "Despite the many all-powerful national deities," Lionel Casson explains, "Egypt's local gods never lost their importance. . . . So in each locale temples arose to house the resident divinity."[8]

Another subgroup of deities included those with dual personalities and roles. Amun-Ra, for example, was the union of the creator god Amun and the sun god Ra. Each still existed as a separate entity. Yet when they merged they formed what was, at least symbolically, a third divine personage. In Wilkinson's words:

> It was as if the Egyptians were acknowledging the presence of one

Osiris, lord of the Underworld, was a major deity. His green skin symbolized fertility.

The Egyptians believed in demons as well as gods. In this painting, a priest confronts three demons, each brandishing a knife.

god or goddess "in" another deity whenever that deity took on a role which was a primary function of the other. But this indwelling does not mean that one deity was subsumed [absorbed] within another, nor does it indicate that the two deities became identical. . . . Rather, the process effectively created a third god where there were originally only two.[9]

Besides the most famous example, Amun-Ra, other dual gods included Khnum-Ra (combining Ra with Khnum, a creation god) and Min-Amun (combining Amun with Min, deity of male sexuality).

Still another way to categorize the Egyptian gods was by their physical appear-ance. Some were seen to assume human shape. Others, which modern scholars call zoomorphic deities, or zoomorphs, took the form of animals, such as falcons, bulls, and lions. A third group, the so-called bimorphs, or hybrids, were half-human and half-animal. The Egyptians did not think these were the gods' actual forms. Such forms were seen as guises assumed by the deities when visiting earth. Their real physical forms were mysterious, even unknowable.

The Divine Cosmos

The places in which the gods dwelled were also fairly mysterious to the Egyptians. The general view was that these deities lived in various parts of the cosmos (universe), including the sky and the Underworld; it was thought that divinities could visit earth by inhabiting a statue in a temple or by some other means. However, there was no way to know exactly where the majority of gods were at any given time, since they were invisible and sometimes worked in mysterious ways.

Nevertheless, the Egyptians developed a reasonably explicit vision of the overall structure of the general realm of the gods—the cosmos. Perhaps because the

Thoth, Master of Knowledge

One of the most important of the ancient Egyptian gods was Thoth. In art he was most often pictured as an ibis or a baboon. And paintings often showed him accompanying the great god Ra on his journey across the sky each day. Thoth began as a moon deity but eventually became associated with writing and knowledge. Richard H. Wilkinson, from his noted book The Complete Gods and Goddesses of Ancient Egypt, *elaborates on Thoth's association with knowledge.*

Thoth was said to have invented the art of writing. He was thus the scribe of the Ennead who recorded "the divine words" and was responsible for all kinds of accounts and records. As "lord of time" and "reckoner of years," he recorded the passing of time and assigned long reigns to kings. He was the patron of all areas of knowledge, and written treatises of all kinds fell under his care as lord of the "houses of life" which functioned as . . . libraries which were attached to the temples. Not surprisingly, then, Thoth commanded magic and secrets unknown to even the other gods and his secret followers were regarded as possessing special knowledge.

This baboon image of the god Thoth once stood at the gate of his temple at Hermopolis.

life-giving waters of the Nile River played so important a role in everyday life in Egypt, water was a central feature of the Egyptian cosmology (description of the cosmos's physical makeup). In fact, it was believed that a dark ocean of water filled the sky and stretched out in all directions infinitely. In the center of all that water was a small bubble that contained earth and its mountains, forests, animals, and people. Only the layer of air now called the atmosphere separated the earthly abode from the vast cosmic waters.

In addition to the sky and earth, the Egyptians recognized a third major sector of the cosmos, which they called the Duat. It lay somewhere beneath the earth and was thought to have its own mountains, forests, and atmosphere. This was where the sun went after it set in the west each day. Somewhere in the Duat could also be found the Underworld, the realm

Ra's manifestation as the morning sun—the hawk-headed Ra-Horakhty—rides the solar boat across the sky in this late New Kingdom painting.

Mummies, Myth, and Magic: Religion in Ancient Egypt

of the dead. An artistic representation of the Egyptian cosmos was discovered on the ceiling of the tomb of the pharaoh Ramesses IV (reigned ca. 1153–1147 B.C.). An accompanying inscription reads:

> The upper side of this sky exists in uniform darkness, the limits of which . . . are unknown, these having been set in the waters, in lifelessness. There is no light . . . no brightness there. And as for every place that is neither sky nor Earth, that is the Duat in its entirety.[10]

Despite the somewhat analytical sound of this passage, the Egyptians' overall view of the cosmos was not a straightforward scientific one, like that which developed in modern times. Instead, as David Silverman points out, "the Egyptian image of the cosmos was usually depicted by using the mythological counterparts of its elements."[11] In other words, the Egyptians thought that invisible divine beings and forces existed within and supported the visible, physical parts of the cosmos. For example, the goddess Nut, the "watery one," was pictured as arching her body over the atmosphere and earth and thereby holding back the sky waters. Her father, Shu, god of air, stood below and helped to support her. At the same time, Shu stood on his son, Geb, the personification of earth and land. (In their roles as water and the earth deities, Nut produced rain when she cried and Geb caused earthquakes when he laughed.)

Perhaps the most important god associated with the visible cosmos was the sun god, Ra (also known as Re). He had many manifestations. To name only two, in the form of the falcon-headed Ra-Horakhty, he represented the morning sun; his evening form, meanwhile, had a ram's head. Eventually, as Amun-Ra, he was recognized as a supreme creator god. Whatever manifestations he assumed, Ra's basic function was cosmological in that he passed across the sky each day and then traversed the Duat at night.

It was believed that Ra rode in a boat in his daily journey across the sky. Other deities who moved through the sky did so as well, since they had to navigate the celestial waters. There were islands in these waters, including the Milky Way—the faint, mistlike patch that runs through several well-known constellations. Others were the so-called fields located in the northerly sector of the sky. Because the stars in that region never set in Egypt and instead circled around a central point, they were thought to be indestructible and eternal. Solar and other divine sky boats could, it was believed, move among these celestial islands.

Other Major Gods

When one considers all of Ra's guises and roles, including that of giving the world light and warmth, he emerges as perhaps the most important, or at least the most versatile, of the gods in the Egyptian pantheon (group or company of gods). But there were a number of other major gods as well. Among them were creator gods, including Atum, Ptah, and Amun. Each of these, depending on the region of the country where his worship originated, was thought to have created the other gods and in some cases animals and humans, too.

Certainly one of the central Egyptian deities was Osiris, who oversaw the realm of the dead. He stood at the gate of his nether kingdom and judged the worthiness of each person trying to enter. Osiris did more than rule the Underworld and afterlife, however. He also made the Nile flood each year, which brought life and prosperity to humankind. In a similar vein, he was a fertility god who made sure that crops and other plants grew and matured.

Because of his importance in sustaining both life on earth and the souls of the dead in the Underworld, Osiris inspired a great deal of diverse and rich iconography in paintings, sculptures, and other visual arts. He was often portrayed as a mummy wrapped in bandages, a reference to his association with the dead. However, his hands were almost always free and held the crook and flail, highly recognizable symbols of Egyptian royalty. (The crook, shaped like a hook, represented the government; the flail, which looked like a small mop on the end of a stick, represented the gods.) Osiris was also commonly shown wearing the *atef*, a white crown shaped somewhat like a bowling pin with a plume attached to either side. Another frequent feature of iconic images of the god was green skin, for the Egyptians associated the color green with fertility and rebirth.

Still another crucial aspect of Osiris's role in cosmic affairs was his relationship with his sister Isis, who also became his wife. Like Osiris, Isis was a fertility goddess. She was particularly associated with the harvesting of wheat and barley, crops essential to Egypt's well-being. Also, she projected the image of a caring, good-hearted mother; her iconography often portrayed her in this role, showing her holding and nurturing her young son, named Horus. In addition, the goddess was thought to forgive people's sins and offer them salvation in the afterlife. A physical description of Isis as she was widely seen in Egypt's Greek and Roman periods was preserved by the Roman writer Apuleius in his novel *The Golden Ass:*

To begin with, she had a full head of hair which hung down, gradually curling as it spreads loosely and flows gently over her divine neck. Her lofty head was encircled by a garland interwoven with diverse blossoms, at the center of which above her brow was a flat disk resembling a mirror, or rather the orb of the moon, which emitted a glittering light. The crown was held in place by coils of rearing snakes . . . and adorned above with waving ears of corn. She wore a multicolored dress woven from fine linen, one part of which shone radiantly white, a second glowed yellow with saffron blossom, and a third blazed rosy red. . . . [A] jet-black cloak gleamed with a dark sheen as it enveloped her. . . . The garment hung down in layers of successive folds, its lower edge gracefully undulating [rippling] with tasseled fringes. . . . Her feet, divinely white, were shod in sandals fashioned from the leaves of the palm of victory. Such, then, was the appearance of the mighty goddess.[12]

Horus, the son of Isis and Osiris, was also a major national god. One of Egypt's earliest known deities, Horus, like Ra, had a large number of manifestations and played a key role in numerous popular myths. One of Horus's images was that of a sky god who took the form of a falcon. Sometimes he was associated directly with the sun god and his rising and setting, in which case he was called "Horus of the two horizons." As Isis's son, Horus possessed the image of a divine, beautiful infant. He was also associated directly with Egypt's royal kingship. An Egyptian pharaoh was thought to be a living manifestation of Horus until he died. As with his divine parents, Horus and his cult spread beyond Egypt to other Mediterranean lands in late antiquity (ancient times). The Greeks called him Harpocrates and saw him as a god of mystery and secret things. In this context, artists showed him as a child holding a finger to his lips, indicating silence and secrecy.

Osiris (at left, wearing the white atef *) greets the spirit of a recently deceased king.*

A Host of Minor Gods

Some Egyptian deities were seen as nearly as important as Isis, Osiris, and Horus. Others, especially local gods, were deemed less important in the grander scheme of things but still demanded respect, fear, and reverence. Some gods or goddesses began as local gods. Then, over time, they fused, or became associated, with similar gods in other areas and thereby gained much wider recognition and acceptance.

A good example of this fusion of divine images and roles is the case of the bovine deity Hathor, goddess of love and beauty and a protector of women. Cow cults seem to have existed in many parts of Egypt in the Predynastic Period, and according to one noted expert "may have been the focus of reverence and veneration even earlier." In fact, the archaeological evidence indicates that cattle were apparently quite important as a source of milk,

blood, and . . . meat in pre-pharaonic cultures that developed in the southern part of Egypt. . . . These benefits . . . may have led early mankind to hold these animals in high esteem. . . . [In time] artisans created sculptures, reliefs, and paintings of Hathor, who was known on a national level . . . [and] to whom the Egyptians dedicated temples.[13]

Hathor began as a local goddess, later gained national recognition, and thereafter people associated or even replaced other local bovine goddesses, such as Bat and Mehet-Weret, with her. Iconic images of Hathor and other bovine goddesses were sometimes zoomorphic, picturing them completely as cows; others were hybrids, depicting them as human bodies with cows' heads or human heads sporting horns.

A number of other gods were commonly pictured as both zoomorphs and hybrids. It has been established that Ra and Horus were associated with falcons. Other deities with falcons' bodies or heads included Montu (a war god who originated in the region of Thebes); Sokar, a protector of craftsmen (from the Memphis region); and Sopdu, "lord of the east," thought to protect Egypt's eastern frontiers from unwanted intruders.

This colorful image of Horus was painted inside the tomb of the pharaoh Horemheb.

Hathor, a bovine goddess, is seen in human form in this New Kingdom painting. She grasps the arm of the hawk-headed Horus.

Praise for a Household Goddess

The Egyptians recognized and worshipped all manner of major and minor divinities. Among the minor gods were several who oversaw the domain of the home, including Ta-Weret, goddess of marriage, birth, and nourishment. The following dedication to the goddess, quoted in A.G. McDowall's Village Life in Ancient Egypt, *was found inscribed on the small doors of a household shrine.*

[I am] giving praise to Ta-Weret, Lady of Heaven . . . lady of nourishment, mistress of [household] provisions, lady of marriage, mistress of the dowry . . . in order that she might give a long life, endurance upon earth, and joy, while my house is richly provided with nourishment such as she gives, while my eyes see her beauty . . . the beautiful character, the kindly one, the beloved of god.

A figurine made of glazed ceramics depicts the kindly household goddess Ta-Weret.

Similarly, there were serpent gods, insect gods, fish gods, and crocodile gods. Of the latter group, the most widely recognized and important was Sobek, whose name came from an Egyptian word meaning "crocodile." Not surprisingly, Sobek was a water god, and it was thought that he ensured the growth and lushness of plants along the riverbank. Like Hathor, Montu, and many other animal gods, Sobek was sometimes pictured as a zoomorph and other times as a hybrid. Often, the priests of cults dedicated to beast deities kept living versions of their animal counterparts within the temples. Herodotus told about seeing sacred crocodiles in two different locations:

In these places they keep one particular crocodile, which they tame, putting rings made of glass or gold into its ears and bracelets round its front feet, and giving it special food and ceremonial offerings. In fact, while these creatures are alive they treat them with every kindness, and, when they die, embalm them and bury them in sacred tombs.[14]

The deities mentioned so far barely scratch the surface of the huge and diverse Egyptian pantheon. Any attempt to examine all of its members would be very time-consuming and potentially confusing. But no matter what an Egyptian god looked like, or what its powers or roles were, or how similar it might be to other deities, all the gods had one underlying attribute in common. Namely, they often acted like humans. And this made it possible for ordinary people to relate to them. As Silverman explains:

> [The gods] thought; they spoke; they dined; and they had emotions. Furthermore, they went into battle and traveled by boat.... [In these and other ways, the gods] became humanized ... [and] organized in such a way that they were comprehensible to most of the population.[15]

Chapter Two

MAJOR CREATION MYTHS

Like other ancient peoples, the Egyptians had a collection of myths that told the stories of their gods and explained how the world came to be. The Egyptian creation myths were unusually diverse and rich. They were also a crucial feature of Egyptian religion. In a society in which religious faith was *the* central cultural aspect, these tales made this deeply religious people feel that both the world and they had a purpose.

Living in the Center of Creation

The creation stories informed the Egyptians that they and the world around them had not always existed; rather, there had been a definite beginning of the cosmos, the world, and the human race. Even the gods themselves were not eternal because they, too, had had a beginning. A collection of religious writings known as the Pyramid Texts states that, in the dim past, "The sky had not yet come into being; the Earth had not yet come into being; humanity had not yet come into being; the gods had not yet been born; death had not yet come into being."[16] Thus, life and existence itself must not be taken for granted, for these had been made possible by the miracle of creation.

The creation stories told the Egyptians two other crucial facts. First, human beings owed their existence to some powerful and mysterious divine beings. And these beings must be repaid for this great and generous act. Dictated by seemingly countless centuries of tradition, this repayment took the form of endlessly repeated rituals of devout worship.

The creation myths also informed the Egyptians that the Nile Valley had been the very focal point of creation. This confirmed for them their already exaggerated sense of their own importance in the world, which had grown in large degree out of their unique geographic situation. Most Egyptians dwelled in a narrow, fertile strip of land running north to south along the fringes of the Nile. Beyond this populated strip stretched many miles of arid deserts, creating a formidable natural barrier. For many centuries the populated regions of Egypt remained more or less isolated from the outside world. So the inhabitants of Egypt came to see themselves as living in the center of creation. They believed that the natural cosmic order revolved around them and their culture and that outsiders were inferior, backward, and not to be trusted. In this way, the Egyptian creation myths reinforced the supposed uniqueness and natural superiority of the Egyptian people and nation.

United by an Underlying Truth

This sense of self-importance had a certain naive logic, given the content of Egypt's creation stories. Less logical was the fact that these tales differed substantially in some of their details, including the matter of which god was central to the creation. In one of these myths the god Atum plays the key role, while others single out Ptah, Amun, or other gods. These and other differences in the stories were the result of the strong local char-acter of Egyptian religion. In the Predynastic Period, each local region developed its personal patron gods and creation stories, which became deeply imbedded in tradition.

However, the Egyptians came to accept all of these myths as equally valid and sacred, in spite of their contradictions. This was partly motivated by political considerations.

Egypt Under the Pharoahs

Mediterranean Sea

LEBANON
Byblos
PALESTINE
Sais
LIBYA
LOWER EGYPT
Tanis
Giza
Memphis
SINAI
Eilat
UPPER EGYPT
el Amarna
Nile River
Abydos
Red Sea
Valley of the Kings
Thebes
Aswan
1st Cataract
Buhen
Abu-Simbel
2nd Cataract
Irrigated Land
3rd Cataract
NUBIA
4th Cataract

GREEKS
Hattusas
HITTITE EMPIRE
Ugarit
Knossos
CRETE
CYPRUS
Kadesh
Memphis
EGYPTIAN EMPIRE (19th dynasty)
THE EGYPTIAN EMPIRE IN THE 13TH CENTURY B.C.

The early pharaohs promoted the multiple creation traditions as a way of being inclusive and thereby maintaining order and obedience among the residents of different sections of the country.

More importantly, however, there was a religious dimension to the acceptance of contradictory creation stories. People did not see them as strictly factual but more in mystical terms. In the words of scholar Vincent A. Tobin, the Egyptians saw these myths as

symbolic statements about phenomena that cannot be fully comprehended by the human intellect. . . . [The myths] were able to preserve the sense of awe and mystery that the Egyptians must have felt when contemplating the surrounding world. . . . [Regardless of the differences in these myths, each] emphasized the fact that there was order and continuity in all things and thus gave the optimistic assurance that the natural, social, and political order would remain stable and secure.[17]

An apt modern analogy would be the acceptance by Christians of the four Gospels of Matthew, Mark, Luke, and John in the Bible's New Testament. These stories of

Ptah, the protector of craftsmen and an important creation god, is shown in mummy wrappings in a painting found in the Valley of the Queens.

Jesus's life and ministry differ in some of their details. Yet all four are seen as equally valid and sacred because most believers see them as varying interpretations of a greater underlying truth. In a like manner, the ancient Egyptians saw a universal truth beneath the details of their own differing creation stories. As Tobin puts it, these myths "bore witness to the unity, harmony, and singleness of everything that exists." [18]

Atum and the Primeval Mound

This underlying unity and singleness is readily apparent in one of the earliest of the major creation myths. This story originated at Heliopolis ("City of the Sun"), the Greek name for the Egyptian Iunu, an important religious center situated about nine miles northeast of the center of modern Cairo. The central god worshipped there was Atum. He was sometimes called Atum-Ra because he was closely associated with, and in some contexts thought actually to be, the sun god, Ra. The priests at Heliopolis viewed Atum as the monad, or the original source of everything, including the other gods. In the temple of Atum, the priests also guarded the sacred *benben*, a stone that represented the original mound of earth created by Atum in the Heliopolitan myth.

In that story, at first there was only a limitless, lifeless ocean. Though lifeless in the sense that there were no animated beings capable of interaction and reproduction, the sea itself was thought to be a being named Nun (or Nu). Atum somehow came into existence within Nun's watery body. In the Pyramid Texts, Atum, in his dual manifestation of Atum-Ra (also called Khepri), says:

> I am he who came into being as Khepri. … I lifted myself from the watery mass, out of inertness [stillness or lifelessness]. I did not find a place where I could stand. I was alone. I took courage in my heart. I laid a foundation. [19]

That foundation was the *benben*, the primeval piece of ground.

Next, Atum created other gods to keep him company. They were twins, Shu and Tefnut, who arose from Atum's bodily fluids. In their turn, Shu and Tefnut created more gods, including Geb, Nut, Osiris, Seth (or Set), Isis, and Nephthys. Together, Atum and the eight other original gods made up a sacred group the Egyptians called the Ennead. The rest of creation followed, including that of humans, who came from another of Atum's bodily fluids. "Men and women," the god says in the same passage of the Pyramid Texts, "arose from tears which came forth from my eye." [20] Atum also fashioned plants and animals.

Creation Through the Spoken Word

A different creation story originated at the Egyptian nation's earliest capital, Memphis, located roughly fifteen miles south of Cairo. The Memphite tradition was centered around the god Ptah, the chief god of that region. Ptah was a god who championed and protected craftsmen. It is not surprising, therefore, as Richard Wilkinson points out, that he became a creator god:

"As the god of metalworkers, craftsmen, and architects, it was natural that Ptah was viewed as the great craftsman who made all things."[21]

Atum, the sacred Ennead, and the primeval mound are prominent in the Memphite creation myth, as they are in the Heliopolitan one. However, as recorded by the Memphite priests on a basalt slab known as the Shabaka Stone (now in the British Museum), Ptah preceded all of these sacred elements. In fact, the Memphite story held that Ptah was the same as Nun, the endless primeval waters. At the same time, in another example of a deity with a dual nature, Ptah was Naunet, a female counterpart of Nun (and Atum's mother).

The most crucial and interesting part of the Memphite myth was the unique manner in which Ptah carried out his acts of creation. He used the powers of his speech; that is, when he named something it immediately materialized. "Every word of the god came into being," the Shabaka Stone inscription contends, "through what the heart mediated and the tongue commanded." Ptah was therefore "the one who had made all things and who had created the gods . . . and from whom all things proceeded."[22]

Scholars and other observers have pointed out that Ptah's use of vocal utterance as a tool of creation closely parallels that of the Judeo-Christian god as depicted in the Bible. "And God said 'Let there be Light'; and there was light,"[23] says a familiar passage from Genesis. And from the Gospel of John comes, "In the beginning was the Word . . . and the Word was God."[24] As Tobin says:

> The Memphite tradition must be regarded as one of the more important products of the Egyptian mind because it . . . [shows] that the Egyptian

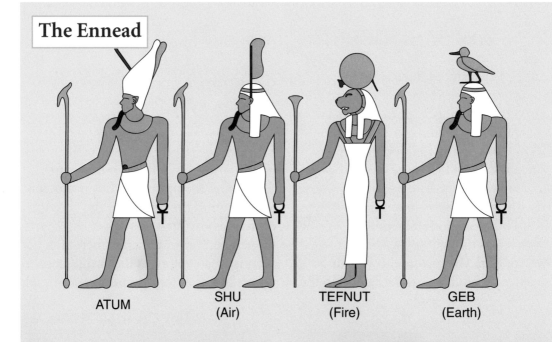

The Ennead

ATUM

SHU
(Air)

TEFNUT
(Fire)

GEB
(Earth)

intellect was capable of dealing with material that would later form the subject of . . . theological speculation in the Jewish and Christian worlds.[25]

The Hermopolitan Tradition

A third Egyptian creation myth emerged from Hermopolis, located approximately 150 miles south of Memphis. The Egyptian name for Hermopolis was Khemnu. In Egyptian, Khemnu means "Town of the Eight," a reference to the eight gods who figure prominently in the local myths of the region. The Egyptians called this group the Ogdoad.

In the Hermopolitan creation story, the members of the Ogdoad were not themselves created. Instead, they already existed, in the form of frogs and snakes, in the dark primeval ocean. The eight gods were divided into four pairs of two, each representing a pivotal characteristic of that

ocean. Nun and Naunet personified the water itself; Hey and Hauhet personified the infinite (since the ocean was supposedly limitless); Kek and Kauket personified darkness; and Amun and Amaunet personified hiddenness.

At some point, as the story goes, these eight deities combined their energies to produce the sun god, Ra (or Atum-Ra). They also gave rise to the primeval mound, which the local priests insisted was located at Hermopolis. According to University of London scholar George Hart, the members of the Ogdoad somehow

interacted explosively and snapped whatever balanced tensions had contained their elemental powers. . . . From the burst of energy released within the churned-up primeval matter, the primeval mound was thrust clear. . . . [It became known as] the Isle of Flame because the Sun god was born on it

NUT (Sky)   OSIRIS   ISIS   SETH   NEPTHYS

and the cosmos witnessed the fiery glow of the first sunrise.[26]

Amun, the Supreme Creator

One member of the Ogdoad—Amun—eventually greatly overshadowed the others. During the later years of the Middle Kingdom (ca. 2055–1650 B.C.) the town of Thebes, situated on the Nile a few hundred miles south of Hermopolis, grew in size and importance. At the dawn of the New Kingdom, it emerged as a national capital and many temples were erected in the area, a number of them dedicated to Amun, usually in his dual role as Amun-Ra. The New Kingdom pharaohs, supported by the powerful priests of Amun at Thebes, promoted Amun-Ra as the country's chief god.

As part of Amun's exalted new status, he came to be seen as an important creator god, one who had somehow predated the other members of the Ogdoad. This was reflected in one of his official titles, the "First One Who Gave Birth to the First Ones." A hymn to Amun-Ra, recorded in a surviving New Kingdom document called the Leiden Papyrus, which came to light in the 1800s, suggests that all other creation gods, including Atum and Ptah, were simply manifestations of Amun:

> The Eight [i.e., the eight deities making up the Ogdoad] were Your first manifestation until You completed these, You being single. Secret was Your body . . . and You kept Yourself hidden as Amun, at the head of the gods. . . . The Ennead combined is Your body.

. . . You emerged first . . . Amun, whose name is hidden from the gods. . . . No god came into being prior to him.[27]

Not surprisingly, just as Amun incorporated several previous gods into his own body and being, his creation story incorporated elements and ideas of the other major creation myths. For example, like Atum, Amun appeared in the dark waters of Nun. When Amun spoke, the explosion of his incredibly loud voice set the rest of creation in motion. First, he made the other seven gods, making up, with him, the Ogdoad; then he transformed himself into the *benben*, the first patch of land on earth. There, he created the nine gods of the Ennead, as well as some other important deities, including the ram-headed god Khnum. Finally, Amun rose into the sky and became the sun god Amun-Ra.

Creation of the Human Race

According to the Theban creation tradition, Amun gave Khnum the task of creating the first humans. The worship of Khnum seems to have originated at Esna, a few miles south of Thebes. There, in the Old Kingdom, he was known mainly for regulating the yearly river floods, but also as a master builder and potter. The first indications of his role as the creator of humans appeared in the Middle Kingdom. And in the New Kingdom, Khnum rose in status to a major creator god working in concert with Amun-Ra, the two acquiring the title the "Lords of Destiny."

In the fully developed New Kingdom creation myth, Khnum began by locating

Mixing Religion and Politics

Through artistic images of the creation myths, Egyptian pharaohs and other leaders often deftly cemented their authority by combining elements of religion with politics. For example, artists often depicted Atum-Ra, the creator sun god, wearing the royal double crown. This crown came into existence when the first pharaoh, Menes, united the kingdoms of Upper and Lower Egypt circa 3100 B.C. Showing Atum-Ra or other gods wearing the double crown suggested that the gods had a direct hand in Egypt's early history and had somehow overseen and approved of the formation of the kingship. This helped later pharaohs to justify the great powers they wielded by making it look as if the political system was somehow sacred and therefore should be honored and perpetuated.

A carved relief from the New Kingdom shows the god Amun blessing a pharaoh.

a special kind of clay. He used it to mold the forms of the first people, then overlaid the clay with vital organs, skin, and so forth. Next, the god breathed into each of the protohumans, thereby infusing them with part of his own life force and giving them the ability to think, walk, and talk.

However, these first people had no place to live, since the primeval mound was still the only land that existed. So Khnum forced the dark waters of Nun back, exposing the expanse of dry land that came to be known as Egypt. He was careful to leave some water, in the form of the Nile River, to sustain his new creations. Finally, the ram-headed god endowed the exposed earth with plants and animals. In this way, the ancient Egyptians believed, the mighty and mysterious act of creation, accomplished in stages by Atum, Ptah, Amun, and other powerful divinities, was at last complete.

Chapter Three

RITUALS TO HONOR THE GODS

ncient Egyptian religion was a very complex institution, with many levels, dimensions, and elements, and it would be close to impossible to sum it up in a single word. But if one had to do so, that word would be *ritual*. Modern religions, including Christianity, Judaism, and Islam, have many traditional rituals, such as attending church, synagogue, or mosque; reciting verses from holy books; and celebrating religious holidays. Yet those who do not always perform these rituals can still claim to be members of said faiths. The key for them is belief. As long as they profess to believe in God and the truth of the formal written precepts of a faith, they are accepted as adherents of that faith.

In contrast, the ancient Egyptians did not base their religious faith on any set of theological principles or on any widely accepted sacred writings, such as the Bible, Torah, or Koran. Instead, their faith was expressed almost entirely by actions, specifically actions that honored and/or pro-

duced some kind of communication with a god or gods. These actions were traditional rituals, all part of the formal cult of one or more gods. Such rituals included the daily care of statues of the gods, making offerings to the deities, attending public festivals to honor the gods, prayer, and so forth. Belief was in effect secondary because nearly everyone believed in the gods without question. The essential issue was the appeasement of the gods, which to be successful required people to perform the rituals.

Why was performing the rituals so important? It was not merely a matter of showing respect for the gods, although that was certainly an important element. The desire of the devout to acquire personal salvation, a crucial motive for worship today, was also secondary. The primary reason for regularly performing rituals was, as Richard Wilkinson says, to ensure "the continuation of existence itself." The Egyptian gods were seen as capable of wiping out humankind at any time they might choose. In fact, one of the major religious stories told how the goddess Hathor went on a spree of mass murder and was stopped from destroying humanity only when her father, Ra, got her so drunk that she fell asleep. Thus, according to Wilkinson, the much larger kind of salvation "was effected through the practice of rituals which supported the gods so that they in turn might be able to preserve and sustain the world"[28] as a stable, harmonious place.

Priests and Their Duties

Today, when most people think of religious rituals, they think of the important role played by clergy, including priests, pastors, rabbis, imams, and other religious leaders. Priests played key roles in ancient Egyptian rituals as well. However, their status and duties were generally very different from those of modern clergy.

First, an Egyptian priest was not a full-time spiritual guide who looked after a congregation of worshippers and dispensed advice to them about how to live. Most priests, especially in the Old and Middle kingdoms, served part-time. They were divided into four groups, which the Egyptians called *saw* ("watches") and the Greeks *phyles* ("gangs"). Members of each group served for a month at a time three times a year, for a total of three months.

In this painting from the tomb of Nefertari, queen of the pharaoh Ramesses II, the queen (right) makes an offering to the goddess Hathor.

During their three months off in each rotation, most went back to their regular jobs. Some people were appointed to the priesthood by the pharaoh. Others inherited their positions from their fathers, and still others, particularly in Egypt's Greek and Roman periods, purchased their positions by giving a temple money or valuables.

The duties of Egyptian priests varied. The most important religious ritual of all was to tend the sacred image of a god in a

A priest dressed in a leopard skin conducts a sacrifice to honor a god.

temple (or elsewhere if the image was moved). In theory, because the pharaoh was officially seen as a god himself, only he had the right to officiate in such matters. In actual practice, however, the pharaoh did not have the time to tend all of the holy images. So he delegated this responsibility to a few high priests, known as "first prophets." Many lesser priests aided the high priests with various tasks. These included helping to wash the sacred images; carrying these images from place to place; helping in sacrifices, such as tending the animals to be sacrificed and cleaning up the mess afterward; and overseeing artists and craftsmen who adorned the temples.

Whatever their duties, all priests had to obey strict rules and cleanliness rituals while in service to a god. Herodotus observed a number of priests during his visit to Egypt and later wrote:

> The priests shave their bodies all over every other day . . . while they are at their religious duties. . . . [They] wear linen only, and shoes made from the papyrus plant—these materials, for dress and shoes, being the only ones allowed them. They bathe in cold water twice a day and twice every night, and observe innumerable other [rules and] ceremonies besides.[29]

Temples and Divine Images

Not surprisingly, priests were most often seen in and around temples, of which Egypt had a great many. These were divided into two general types—mortuary tem-

Priests carve up a bull following a sacrifice. It was a common custom for those who had witnessed the ceremony to take part in a ritual feast.

ples and cult temples. A mortuary temple was intended as a memorial to and spiritual aid for a king or queen. The priests who staffed a mortuary temple prayed and made offerings in order to nourish and sustain the monarch's spirit in the afterlife. A cult temple, by contrast, was built and maintained for the direct worship of one or more gods. Unlike modern churches, synagogues, and mosques, Egyptian temples were not places for average people to gather and worship. With the exception of some outer courtyards of temples on a few special occasions each year, access to the interiors of these buildings was restricted to royalty, a few high-placed nobles, and priests.

The focal point of a temple was the sacred image of a god, which had to be tended with the utmost care. Although the layout of temples varied, almost all had the holy of holies—the chamber (or in some cases chambers) containing the divine statue(s)—in a rear section. This area was kept off limits to all but a select few and was well guarded.

The Egyptians did not view the sacred cult image, which was made of stone, metal, or wood, as the god itself, a common misconception. Rather, it was thought that a manifestation or part of the divinity inhabited the image. Therefore, it was important to treat the statue as if it were alive. This treatment consisted of daily rituals in which priests removed the image from the shrine, washed it, and dressed it in fresh clothes. In addition, scholar Stephen E. Thompson explains:

> The god was presented with various objects, such as his crowns, scepter, [and] crook and flail. . . . Next the god's face was anointed [with holy water], sand was scattered around the chapel, the cult image was replaced in the shrine, and the door-bolt was thrown and sealed. Finally, the priest . . . exited the sanctuary, dragging a broom behind him to obliterate his footprints.[30]

Offerings to the Gods

In addition to these traditional daily rituals, it was seen as essential to make various kinds of material offerings to a god. One type of offering provided a deity with nourishment in the form of cow, sheep, goat, or bird meat; crops such as grains, fruits, or vegetables; or liquids like milk, wine, or honey. Some of these food offerings were placed before the divine image. It was obvious that the god did not consume them directly, since they were still there when the priests entered the sanctuary the next day. The belief was that a deity absorbed the "essence" of the food, leaving the material part behind. The priests then divided and ate the food, the older and more experienced among them getting the choicest items.

Some nourishment was also offered to the gods through sacrifice, in which animals were ritually slaughtered and parts of them burned, a practice common throughout the ancient world. Herodotus observed some Egyptian sacrifices and later described them. He emphasized that the priests had to follow strict rules during all stages of the ritual. Before sacrificing a bull, for example:

> A priest appointed for the purpose examines the animal, and if he finds a single black hair on him, pronounces him unclean [not fit for the sacrifice]. He goes over him with the greatest care, first making him stand up, then lie on his back. . . . He also inspects the [tongue and the] tail. If the animal passes all the tests successfully, the priest marks him. . . . They take the beast . . . to an appropriate altar and light a fire; then, after pouring a libation [liquid sacrifice] of wine and invoking the god by name, they slaughter it, cut off its head, and flay [cut up] the carcass. . . . When they have finished cutting up the bull, they stuff the body with loaves of bread, honey, raisins, figs . . . and other nice-smelling substances. Finally, they pour a quantity of oil over the body and burn it. . . . While the fire is consuming it, they beat their breasts.[31]

Priests carve up a bull following a sacrifice. It was a common custom for those who had witnessed the ceremony to take part in a ritual feast.

Like other ancient peoples, the Egyptians believed that the smoke from the burning animal rose up and nourished the god. After the sacrifice, the priests sliced the animal into small portions and served these to any worshippers who might be watching the ceremony.

Another type of offering made to the gods was called a votive offering. It was not intended to nourish or appease a god but to accompany a request for a favor or to thank the god for granting said favor. Some votive offerings took the form of food, drink, or flowers. Small figurines of gods or kings—made of wood, pottery, or metal—were also popular gifts. These were at first hand-made, but in the eras following the New Kingdom the demand for such images grew so great that they were mass-produced by artisans. Requests or thanks for favors were also carved or painted in writing onto stelae and presented to the gods. In the New Kingdom it became common practice to draw or carve one or more human ears on a stele to make sure the deity "heard" the message.

Religious Festivals

Making votive and other offerings to the gods was one of the principal forms of ritual activity engaged in by Egyptians of all walks of life. Another was taking part in annual religious festivals. It is difficult to ascertain the exact number of religious festivals held throughout Egypt's long history. Lists of them on the walls of temples dating to the New Kingdom count as many as

Isis's Ship-Launching Festival

Among the most popular religious festivals in ancient Egypt were those honoring the goddess Isis. One, the Festival of Seeking and Finding, included a reenactment of her search for the parts of Osiris's body after Seth murdered him and cut him up. The other festival, called the Launching of Isis's Ship, celebrated the coming of spring and the renewal of life that accompanies it. In his novel The Golden Ass, *the Roman writer Apuleius describes the ship ceremony as it took place in his own time in the second century* A.D.

The chief priest names and consecrates to the goddess a ship which has been built with splendid craftsmanship.... Holding a flaming torch, he first pro- nounces most solemn prayers . . . and then with an egg and sulfur he performs over it an elaborate ceremony of purification.... Then the entire population, devotees and uninitiated alike, vie in piling the ship high with baskets laden with spices and similar offerings, and they pour on the waves libations [liquid offerings] of meal soaked in milk. Eventually the ship, filled with generous gifts . . . is loosed from its anchor-ropes and launched on the sea before a friendly, specially appointed breeze. Once its progress has caused it to fade from sight, the bearers of sacred objects . . . make their eager way back to the temple.

Ornate boats like the one in this early modern painting were used in Isis's festivals.

sixty. A few of these were big national festivals; the rest were regional or local affairs.

Of the national holidays, one of the oldest and more important was the New Year Festival. It was held on July 19, the first day of the year on the civil calendar. This was also the day that Sirius, the brightest star in the sky, rose at a set point on the horizon, coinciding with the start of the Nile's annual flood.

Equally important but larger in scale was the Festival of Opet, which rose to prominence during the New Kingdom. Celebrated in the second month of the flood season, it lasted from two to four weeks and drew enormous crowds to the capital of Thebes. There, on the eastern bank of the Nile, a solemn but opulent and colorful procession took place. Accompanied by many musicians and worshippers, priests carried portable boats in which the sacred images of three gods rested. One was the supreme god, Amun-Ra; the others were his consort, Mut, and son, Khonsu. The procession bore the statues from the huge temple complex of Karnak southward through an avenue lined by stone sphinxes to the temple of Luxor, erected specifically for this celebration.

Such processions were only one aspect of the festivals, especially the larger ones. People also prayed, danced, sacrificed, feasted, and in general socialized and enjoyed themselves. Some idea of these and other festival activities comes from paintings and carved reliefs on temple walls. A few eyewitness accounts by Greek and Roman writers have survived as well. Herodotus described part of the celebration attending the worship of Neith (whom he tried to equate with the Greek Athena), a creator and mother goddess popular in the Nile Delta. "On the night of the sacrifices," he wrote,

> everybody burns a great number of lights in the open air around the houses. The lamps they use are flat dishes filled with [olive] oil and salt, with a floating wick which keeps burning throughout the night. The festival is called the Festival of Lamps, and even Egyptians who cannot attend it mark the night of the sacrifice by lighting lamps, so that on that night lamps are burning . . . throughout the country.[32]

Communication with the Divine

During festivals, and also at other times of the year, worshippers took part in rituals that would hopefully involve direct communication between themselves and a god. The most common way, as remains true in modern religions, was through prayer. Many prayers began with generic recitations that followed set formulas. Similar to the modern "Hail Mary, full of grace," they often addressed the god by name and mentioned some important attribute it was known for, for example: "Hail to you Ra, Lord of Truth." Then came various praises of the deity, followed by the person's request, if any. Typical were requests for bountiful harvests, finding a suitable husband or wife, recovery from an illness, and victory in battle. The following surviving prayer to the sun god by a pharaoh of the First Intermediate Period, Intef II (reigned 2112–2063 B.C.), asks simply for the courage to get through dark and scary nights: "[O Ra,] commend me to the night and those dwelling in it . . . [I], who worships you at your risings, who laments at your settings. May night embrace me by your command."[33]

Another way to communicate with the divine was through oracles. In the ancient world, oracles were people or statues that supposedly acted as mediums, or conduits, for questions and answers between a god and a human. The most common form of oracle in Egypt was a sacred image of a deity. Ordinary petitioners might gain access to such a statue during a festival

A statue of the god Anubis rests on a litter used to carry the image in sacred processions.

when priests carried it outside a temple. Evidence suggests that when someone asked a question, the answer was indicated by the movement of the litter on which the god's image rested; forward movement of the litter meant "yes," backward movement meant "no."

Still another way to communicate with a god was through dreams. In a process known as incubation, a deity either visited the person in his or her dream or revealed the future through the events of the dream. A surviving manuscript called the *Dream Book*, possibly written in the thirteenth century B.C., lists the meanings of various dream events. If someone dreamed of seeing a big cat, it indicated that a plentiful harvest was on the way; killing an ox was a sign that one's enemies would go away; falling was a sign of impending prosperity; being bitten by a dog was a sign that someone had placed a magic spell on the dreamer; and drinking wine indicated that the dreamer was a righteous person.

Seeking Cosmic Harmony

That the average Egyptian took such dream interpretations seriously is very revealing of the state of mind of Egyptian society as a whole. People saw incubation, along with regular and earnest prayer, making offerings, attending festivals, and other religious rituals and practices, as a way to reach harmony with divine forces. The belief was that if one failed to do so, nature's

Lodging a Complaint to a God

It was common custom in ancient Egypt for people of various walks of life to petition one or more gods through oracles. The following surviving petition (quoted in A.G. Mc-Dowall's Village Life in Ancient Egypt*) dates from the Twentieth Dynasty (ca. 1186–1069 B.C.). The identity of the petitioner and the nature of his request are somewhat unclear, but it appears that he was a merchant who had a dispute with an official (the vizier) over delivery of some clothes items. The petition seems to be a complaint that the deity has not seen fit to settle the dispute.*

I was looking for you to tell you some matters of mine, but you happened to be hidden in your sanctuary and there was no one [i.e., no nonpriest] admitted to send it to you. . . . You will cast off mystery today and come out in the course of a procession, so that you may judge the matters of the five kilts of the temple of Horemheb and these further two kilts of the scribe of the Necropolis. The vizier will not take the clothes, saying, "until you make up their number!" . . . You do not send me either good or bad [messages]. Behold, you caused there to be eleven [kilts?] for Isis . . . while [now] it happens that your voice does not come [to help settle the dispute]. . . . Farewell.

balance might tip against him or her or society in general. David Silverman sums up the importance of these rituals and practices in Egyptian life this way:

> A permanent tension [was thought to exist] between cosmic opposites, such as good and bad, light and dark . . . and above all, between . . . harmonious order and chaos. . . . It followed in the Egyptian mind that mortals should seek to ensure, through their rituals, the continuation of cosmic order and the benevolence of the gods.[34]

Chapter Four

Magic Spells and Amulets

The ancient Egyptians believed that no matter which creator god one singled out—Atum, Ptah, Amun, or another—that deity was possessed and empowered by a mystical divine force called *heka*. Sometimes people personified that force as a separate god named Heka. However one characterized the force, the widespread belief was that under certain circumstances it could be called forth to solve problems or to harm or protect individuals or groups. The modern word for *heka* and its various uses by humans is *magic.*

Today, few people take the concept of magic seriously, and it lies on the extreme fringes of intellectual activity, discredited by scientists and most other educated people. In contrast, the Egyptians took magic very seriously and viewed it as overlapping with or equal in status to major, accepted categories of knowledge such as medicine and astronomy, as well as to core rituals such as prayer. Partly for this reason, magic

was not seen as sinister or evil as it often is today. Instead, it was an accepted part of the Egyptians' overall belief system, which also included divine beings and the rituals associated with them.

In fact, it was common practice to invoke the name of a god or goddess to make magic work. This was based on the notion that only gods possessed *heka* and therefore only through a god could that force be properly channeled. The two deities most often called on were Hathor and Isis. But all of the others were invoked at one time or another.

The main reason Isis was singled out so often was that some of the myths associated with her contained episodes in which she successfully used magic to get her way. In one of the most famous of these mythical episodes, the great god Ra was bitten by a poisonous serpent and became so ill that he could not speak. In the story, "His lips were quivering and all his limbs were trembling." But luckily for him, "Isis came with her magic power. Her utterance possesses the breath of life, her speech dispels suffering, her words revive the one whose throat is constricted."[35]

Thus, magic and religion were closely related. Still, in the case of humans practicing magic, there were some significant differences between the two disciplines. First, when a person engaged in magic he or she, and not a god, caused something to happen. Second, religion was not always a means to an end, whereas magic was. As noted Egyptologist Bob Brier writes:

> In religious ritual, such as prayer, there is often an ultimate goal in sight, but the goal is not essential. It is possible to worship a god just for the sake of worshiping the god. The worshiper does not have to be asking for something. In magic this is not possible. A magician never recites a spell for its own sake—magic is never an end in itself, it is always a means to an end. Magic is a direct attempt by the practitioner to control supernatural forces to achieve a specific goal.[36]

Magicians and Their Art

Who were these magicians who attempted to control and manipulate supernatural forces? Perhaps not surprisingly, most of them were priests, the most respected religious authorities in society. It was they who were seen to have the strongest connections with the gods who possessed the essential and potent force of *heka*.

Not all priests were magicians, however. It appears that most of this subclass of priests worked in the House of Life. A building or chamber found on the grounds or within the walls of every temple, the House of Life was a sort of library that contained written documents. These documents included stories about and hymns to the gods, chants, spells, mystical manuscripts such as the *Dream Book*, and so forth. In a sense, the priests of the House of Life were keepers of knowledge; and in a society in which the vast majority of

Isis was often invoked in magic spells because she was known for using magic herself.

people could not read, these men held considerable power and inspired great respect, even awe. They had the prestigious task of using magic to protect the pharaoh and royal family. Also, for a fee the priest-magicians helped ordinary people invoke magic.

There is little doubt that some of these powerful men took advantage of their lofty status for selfish motives or to maintain the prestigious reputation of their religious order. To these ends, they likely developed various tricks of the trade such as sleight of hand and other illusions like those employed by modern show business magicians. As Brier suggests, evidence for this can be found in the Bible:

When Moses and Aaron went before the pharaoh to ask him to let the Israelites leave Egypt, they intended to impress the pharaoh with their power. To do this, Aaron threw down a staff. It turned into a serpent, but the pharaoh was unimpressed, evidently because he had seen such tricks before. He called on his magicians to do the same, and their rods, too, turned into serpents. It is possible that the trick of turning a staff into a serpent was a standard effect used by magicians in the ancient Near East.[37]

A smaller group of magicians consisted of nonpriestly, or "lay," practitioners.

Ancient Egyptian vs. Modern Religion

Unlike Christianity and other modern faiths, which reject magic, ancient Egyptian religion accepted magic without question. In this passage from his book on Egyptian religion, Fordham University scholar Byron E. Shafer comments on this and other contrasts between that faith and most modern ones.

Many people today find life's meaning outside of religion and view religion as incidental or tangential to [a minor aspect of] life; very few ancient Egyptians saw it this way. Of today's devout, all but a few are monotheists [believers in a single god]; of ancient Egypt's, all but a few were polytheists [believers in many gods]. . . . We hold omnipotence [having all power] and omniscience [having all knowledge] as necessary attributes of divinity; they did not. We have a canon of scripture [such as the Bible or Koran]; they did not. We reject magic; they did not. We view government as secular [nonreligious] and rulers as all too human; they saw government as sacred and kings as somehow divine. We believe that the world needs to be improved, and therefore (if we are religious) to be transformed by communal obedience to God's revealed will; they believed that the world needs to be maintained, and therefore to be stabilized by governmental imposition of order from above.

Very little is known about them. The general consensus among scholars is that they were probably similar to modern faith healers and fortune tellers who claim to possess special insights or powers that put them in touch with divine forces. But whether priest or layman, all Egyptian magicians used the same basic approach to magic. Their art involved two essential elements—spell and ritual. The spell consisted of a series of words that had to be recited properly and precisely. The ritual was some action that accompanied the spell. Such rituals included burning incense, waving magic wands, dancing, drinking potions, making and/or breaking wax or pottery images, and many others.

As the pharaoh watches, Aaron's staff turns into a serpent.

Magic Used as a Weapon

The making and breaking of images was a central feature of one common type of magic, namely the kind that a person used to harm a personal enemy. The magician fashioned an image, usually in the form of a small pottery or wax figurine, which represented the enemy. Or sometimes he used existing statues of a specific person. Then, while reciting an appropriate spell, the magician mutilated or smashed the image. A variation that was also often used was to write the enemy's name on an ostracon

(broken piece of pottery) and then smash it. It was thought that marring the image indirectly hurt the enemy.

Harmful spells could also take the form of written curses designed to damage or thwart one's enemies. A number of such curse-spells have survived. In one, the instigator of the magic says that he will be like a fly, which, because of its tiny size, can invade the enemy's privacy, even his body:

I am the one who enters the sleeping place [the enemy's bed?]. . . . I will enter your belly as a fly, and I will see your belly from the inside. I will turn your face into the back of your head; the front of your foot into your heel. Your speech is no use [i.e., words will not help you]; it will not be heard. Your body will be weak and your knee will be feeble.[38]

Such harmful spells could be used against anyone. In fact, surviving records show that a small group of conspirators even had the audacity to try to bring down a pharaoh through the use of such magic. This has come to be known as the "Harem Conspiracy" because it indirectly involved some of the wives of the pharaoh Ramesses III (reigned 1184–1153 B.C.). The conspirators, members of Ramesses' court, managed to get personal information about the king from these wives. Next they got the head of the palace library to supply a formula for a magical spell, which likely had originated in the House of Life of a nearby temple. The conspirators then added the personal information to the words of the formula to focus the power of the magic directly on the king. They also made and mutilated wax figures of Ramesses. In the end, all of these efforts were in vain, for the pharaoh discovered the scheme and severely punished those involved.

A priest (at left) sprinkles holy water with his right hand. The idea of holy water having curative or magical properties is still common today.

Magic Used to Heal

Egyptian magic was used to heal as well as to hurt. There were three general categories of physician in Egypt: priest doctors, lay doctors, and magician doctors. Members of the latter group exclusively employed magic to heal. The other two kinds of physician performed surgery and prescribed medicine (usually herbs) but also relied on magic as a supplementary approach. Most of the surviving Egyptian medical documents consist of magical cures.

As harmful magic did, healing magic combined spells with physical actions. For example, if one wanted to dispel disease, which was thought to be caused by demons, one could obtain a stick, or magic wand, from a specific kind of tree and carry it around and around the outside of the house. It was believed that this would create a circle of protection that, strengthened by the recitation of the following spell, would keep sickness out:

> Withdraw, you disease demons. The wind shall not reach me, that those who pass by may pass by to work disaster against me. I am [i.e., I am channeling the power of] Horus, who passes by the diseased one [and is healthy]. . . . I am the unique one, son of Bastet [a cat-headed goddess known for her protective powers]. I die not through you.[39]

To protect oneself from scorpion stings, a person could recite the same spell and use a wand to draw a circle around his or her bed.

Magic spells could also be mixed with home remedies and other concoctions to facilitate healing. For example, to rid someone of cataracts (obstructions in the lens of the eye), one said a certain spell while mixing a turtle's brain with honey. This mixture was then applied to one or both eyes. To cure a headache, one could say the appropriate spell while mixing specific fish products with onions, honey, and other ingredients and then rubbing this mixture on the head.

Another magical approach to healing was the use of holy water, that is, water that had been magically transformed by contact with the divine. For instance, at Dendera, not far north of Thebes, the major local temple had a corridor lined with statues of gods, each carved with spells associated with healing. Priests poured water over the statues and the now sanctified water drained into small tubs or pools. Hoping to be cured, sick people came and bathed in these pools. In a similar vein, water poured over statues of Horus as a child was thought to have curative powers when drunk.

Magic Used for Protection

Another important beneficial use of magic was to protect a person from potential harm. This was accomplished mainly by wearing or carrying amulets, various objects thought to possess positive magical properties. These were by far the most prevalent magical aids used by the Egyptians, as evidence suggests that almost everyone wore or carried some kind of amulet most of the time.

Amulets were made from a wide range of materials, including many kinds of stone (feldspar, turquoise, and lapis lazuli among the more popular); metals (gold, copper, bronze, and iron); wood; bone; and, most popular of all, faience, paste made from ground quartz that could be molded into any shape and baked so that it had a smooth, glassy surface.

Amulets were thought to acquire their protective powers in several ways. One was through invoking the blessings of a god, which was accomplished by fashioning the amulet in the form of that god. A person might gain protection from Bastet, for example, by wearing an amulet shaped like a cat. Other amulets derived their powers from potent symbols. One such symbol was the ankh, which was shaped like a cross with a small oval loop at the top. Because the ankh stood for "life," wearing an ankh amulet might help ensure continued life or health. The most popular of the symbolic amulets was that of the so-called Eye of Horus. According to a popular myth, Horus's eye was mutilated during a battle with another god, after which Thoth, god of knowledge, collected the pieces and put them back together. The amulet representing these reassembled pieces was called an *udjat* (meaning "sound eye"). Because it symbolized healing through regeneration, it was believed to promote continued health.

Another very popular amulet was the scarab, shaped like the beetle of the same name. Scarabs derived their protective powers in various ways, as Brier explains:

The Egyptians were especially fond of puns, and the hieroglyphs [written picture signs] for beetle . . . also meant "to exist." So if you wore a scarab amulet, your continued existence was assumed. Another reason the scarab was held in special regard is that the ancient Egyptians believed [incorrectly] that the beetle had offspring without the union of male and female. . . . They assumed the beetle was somewhat like the god Atum, who begot children without a female partner. . . . [Also] when the scarab fashions [a] dung ball it rolls it with its hind legs to a sunny place. To the ancient mind, this in some way resembled the journey of the Sun across the sky.[40]

Still another kind of magical protection widely employed in ancient Egypt was the papyrus amulet, which became popular in the centuries following the New Kingdom. Essentially, it consisted of a drawing and written message on a small piece of papyrus parchment. Because the vast majority of people were not literate, most of those who wanted such an amulet went to a magician. He drew a picture of the god whose powers were being invoked on the parchment and also wrote the god's name, an essential element because gods were always addressed and invoked by name. Words linking the god to the owner of the amulet were then added.

Papyrus amulets were frequently used to protect children. After a magician had prepared the parchment, it was folded or rolled up and placed inside a small wooden

These ancient amulets, on display at Berlin's Egyptian Museum, include a Horus falcon (lower left) and a head of the god Bes (lower right).

The Mysterious Ankh Symbol

In this excerpt from his informative book about ancient Egyptian magic, Long Island University scholar Bob Brier discusses the meaning and origin of the ankh, one of the most popular ancient Egyptian symbols, which was occasionally used for amulets.

The word *ankh* meant both "life" and "hand mirror." Tutankhamun ["King Tut"] had a mirror in the shape of an *ankh*, a pun any Egyptian would have gotten. There are two curious aspects to the *ankh*. First, although it was a symbol frequently used in painting and sculpture, the objective evidence is that it was used as an amulet only rarely. Comparatively few have been found in excavations. . . . The second curiosity about the *ankh* is that . . . Egyptologists are not certain just what object it represented. Some believe that it represented sandal straps, while this is far from certain. The fact that there was no

particular material from which *ankhs* were to be made indicates that the origins may have been lost even to the Egyptians.

The ankh symbol is central to this stele from Osiris's temple at Abydos.

or leather container. The child wore the container around his or her neck. The text of a papyrus amulet now on display in the British Museum reads in part that the god promises "to keep him [the child] healthy in his flesh and his bones. I shall keep healthy his head." The deity also pledges to "keep healthy" the boy's eyes, teeth, tongue, nose, belly, lungs, liver, and other body parts and to "enable him to grow up."[41] Such surviving examples of amulets and other objects and writings associated with magic underscore the crucial role played by this mystical branch of knowledge and religion in everyday Egyptian life.

Chapter Five

BELIEFS ABOUT THE AFTERLIFE

"No civilization ever devoted so much of its energies and resources to the quest for immortality as did Egypt's,"[42] remarks Egyptologist Bob Brier. Indeed, belief in an afterlife and concerted efforts to reach the mysterious realm of the dead after one died played central roles in the lives of Egyptians of all walks of life. The reason people were so preoccupied with these matters was the widespread belief that making it to the afterlife was not automatic. Rather, one had to accomplish much in the present life to ensure survival in the next life. It was important to behave morally during one's earthly existence since the gods stationed at the gates to the Underworld would judge a person worthy or unworthy of entry. Also, one needed to make preparations for proper preservation and burial of the body. This stemmed from the traditional belief that the body must be preserved to support the continued existence of at least part of the soul.

Immortality for All

Interestingly, evidence suggests that most Egyptians were not as preoccupied with these things in Egypt's earliest centuries. It appears that during the Predynastic Period and the first centuries of the Old Kingdom the view was that only the pharaoh was granted immortality. This seemed natural because he was supposedly the manifestation of a god living in a human body. Those who directly attended the king—his wives, leading nobles, and servants—might be allowed immortality because he needed them to help sustain him in the afterlife. All others were excluded from the benefits of life after death.

Over time, however, this belief system that favored a few fortunate rich individuals and their servants changed and the opportunity for entry into the afterlife was extended to all. As Lionel Casson puts it:

Immortality was democratized as it were, and every Egyptian in the land,

The body of a deceased person lies near the funerary barge that will convey him in his journey in the afterlife.

high or humble, came to consider himself eligible for eternal life after death. This was certainly the case by Middle Kingdom times. [High social status] and the income that went with it gave a man a fine burial and an elaborate tomb, but such things meant only a higher degree of post-mortem comfort. . . . Now prayers and rites and way of life were what gained one [access] to immortality, and these were at the disposal of everybody.[43]

Thus, throughout most of recorded times in ancient Egypt, a majority of Egyptians believed they could reach the afterlife and hoped that they would. This did not mean that they expected it to be better than life on earth, however. Here is one of several areas in which ancient

Egyptian beliefs differ widely from those of most modern religions. Christians and Muslims, for example, often speak about going to a "better place" after they die. They generally picture the positive portion of the afterlife, heaven, as a place devoid of earthly ills, cares, wants, and confusions.

In comparison, the Egyptians had a somewhat less optimistic and more practical view. They thought that earthly life simply continued in the afterlife; for example, a farmer expected to remain a farmer in the next life, with the same daily tasks and duties. If in his earthly life he worked part-time on the pharaoh's building projects, he could expect to do the same in the afterlife. But at least there was the consolation that there would be no pain or suffering in the world beyond.

The Parts of the Soul

One important difference between earthly life and the afterlife for the Egyptian was the form a person took in these places. On earth, of course, people existed in material bodies. In the afterlife, by contrast, the belief was that they would exist as souls.

More specifically, *parts* of their souls would inhabit various stages of the afterlife, since the Egyptians held that the soul was a conglomerate made up of several parts. Scholarly opinions differ somewhat on how many parts of the soul existed and how each functioned. But the general consensus is that there were five parts: the *ka*, *ba*, *akh*, name, and shadow. Perhaps the most important, at least in the time period immediately following death, was the

ka. According to English Egyptologist A. Rosalie David, this was

the person's life force, which acted as his guide and protector from birth

The Negative Confession

Following are some of the thirty-six denials of the famous "negative confession" (translated in volume 2 of Miriam Lichtheim's Ancient Egyptian Literature*), which was spoken to the god Osiris by a petitioner attempting to enter the Underworld.*

I have not done crimes against people. I have not mistreated cattle. I have not sinned in the Place of Truth [a temple or cemetery]. I have not known what should not be known. I have not done any harm. I did not begin a day by exacting more than my due [demanding more than I deserved]. . . . I have not caused tears. I have not killed. . . . I have not ordered [anyone else] to kill. I have not made anyone suffer. . . . I have not depleted the loaves of the gods [i.e., stolen food offerings intended for deities]. I have not stolen the cakes of the dead. . . . I have not taken milk from the mouths of children. . . . I have not quenched a needed fire. I have not neglected the days of meat offerings. . . . I have not stopped a god in his procession. No evil shall befall me in this land, in this Hall of the Two Truths; for I know the names of the gods in it, the followers of the great God!

onward. During life this was sometimes regarded as his double and thought to incorporate all the qualities and characteristics that make an individual unique. Essentially, it was the "self" or personality. On death the *ka* separated from the body. . . . [But it] still retained a vital link with the preserved body and depended on the food offering brought to the tomb.[44]

Another vital part of the soul was the *ba*. Like the *ka*, it was an aspect of the person's personality. But unlike the *ka*, which always remained near the body in the tomb or grave, the *ba* could separate, leave the grave, and go virtually anywhere it wanted. Some

bas were thought to ascend into the sky, where they became stars. But a common belief was that a person's *ba* often visited the places that he or she frequented in life. It was also thought that the *ba* retained humanlike needs, including eating and sexual activity.

The other parts of the soul were related to the *ka* and *ba* in certain ways. The *akh* was the "effective" manifestation of the soul, that is, the form the soul took once it reached the Underworld. The *ka* and *ba* could not make it to the Underworld by themselves, and only when they were united in the *akh* could the person go ahead with his or her regular activities in the Underworld. A fourth part of the soul, the name, was the unique quality that identified the dead person as distinct from

The god Osiris (left) watches as Anubis weighs the heart of a deceased person. The grim judges who assisted Osiris are seated above.

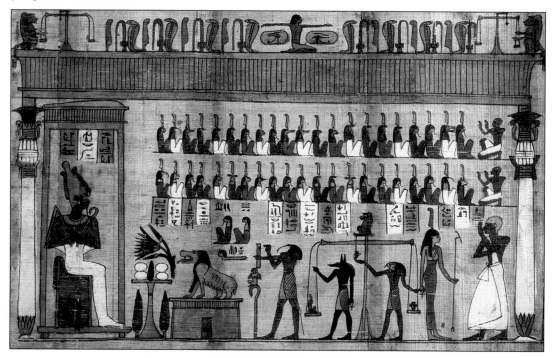

Another depiction of the ritual weighing of a dead person's heart (in the jar on the right side of the scale) appears in the tomb of a nobleman.

all others seeking entrance into the afterlife. And the fifth part, the shadow, was thought to protect the other parts of the soul from harm.

Judgment of the Dead

This description of the various parts of the soul emphasizes that the deceased person did not necessarily make it into the Underworld immediately after death. Rather, there might be an undetermined span of time before this happened. What happened during this period is somewhat unclear. But apparently part of the time was spent in the judgment phase.

The judgment consisted of the deceased person appearing before Osiris, lord of the Underworld, and a group of supernatural juror-judges who assisted him. When society first began to accept that ordinary Egyptians could gain immortality, it became understood that a person had to prove to these deities that he or she had led an ethical life. Perhaps people did not like the idea of simply taking their chances of convincing Osiris of their righteousness. In any case, specific words and speeches designed to help better those chances evolved. They became a complex system of spells, prayers, and chants that people wrote down and eventually collected into a funerary text; today it is known as the Book of the Dead, although the Egyptian name for it translates roughly as "the spell for coming forth by day."

The most crucial portion of this text is often called the "negative confession," which is a series of statements, each swearing that a specific sin had not been committed. It was expected that the deceased individual petitioning to enter the Underworld would recite the confession to Osiris and the other divine judges. So people often memorized the statements at some point in their life. But to make sure that the deceased would not forget any of them, during the final ceremonies in the tomb or at the gravesite relatives commonly placed a written copy between the corpse's legs. The negative confession reads in part:

> I have not done crimes against people.
> I have not mistreated cattle. I have not sinned in the Place of Truth [a temple or cemetery]. . . . I have not blasphemed [spoken against] a god. I have not robbed the poor. I have not done what the god abhors [hates]. . . . I have not caused tears. I have not killed. . . . I have not damaged the offerings in the temples. . . . I have not taken milk from the mouths of children. . . . I have not held back water in its season. I have not dammed a flowing stream.[45]

After reciting thirty-six of these denials, the petitioner would begin to address Osiris's forty-two assistants one by one. These grim characters bore such ominous names as "Flame-grasper," "Bone-smasher,"

"Blood-eater," and "Fiend from the slaughterhouse." The deceased issued a denial of sin to each of these jurors; for example: "O Blood-eater who comes from the slaughter place, I have not slain sacred cattle."[46]

Finally, after a total of seventy-eight denials, the petitioner launched into a list of his or her charitable works. Typical examples were clothing the naked and feeding the hungry. Another ceremony described in the Book of the Dead, as well as in surviving tomb paintings, was the weighing of the petitioner's heart. Osiris presided, the jackal-headed god Anubis operated the scale, and Thoth, divine scribe, recorded the results. Supposedly, if the deceased had lied to the gods in the confessions, the heart would reveal it by tipping the scale the wrong way.

The Fate of the Dead

One common belief was that if the petitioner did not pass these tests, he or she was promptly fed to a hideous monster. Called the Swallower of the Damned, it lurked nearby, ready and eager to annihilate any and all sinners. An alternate view was that the damned were not dispatched immediately but went on suffering in a hell-like existence. In the grave, "demons tear away their mummy wrappings," Dutch scholar J.V. Dijk writes,

> and uncover their bodies, which are left to decompose. In the place to which they are condemned . . . the damned have to walk upside down, eat their own excrement, and drink their

own urine. . . . Their heads and limbs are severed from their bodies and their flesh is cut off their bones; their hearts are taken out; their *ba*-souls are separated from their bodies, forever unable to return to them. . . . They have no air and suffer from hunger and thirst. . . . Worst of all, they are denied the reviving light of the Sun god, who ignores them.[47]

On the other hand, if the petitioner passed the tests administered at the gates of the Underworld, he or she was allowed to enter. Ancient Egyptian literary and artistic depictions of this nether realm varied. In the most optimistic version it appeared as the "Field of Rushes," a pleasant place existing somewhere in the east, where the sun rises. It was not a paradise, like the Christian and Muslim heaven. But it had abundant fields, water, air, and so forth, so the souls of the dead could engage in the same pursuits they had on earth.

Another common view was that a person's *ba* passed through the Field of Rushes temporarily once each day. In this vision of the afterlife, each day the *ba* left the body (which remained in the grave or tomb), ascended into the sky, and joined with Ra,

Appeasing Osiris's Judges

After reciting the negative confession, the petitioner trying to gain entry into the Underworld made declarations to each of Osiris's forty-two assistant judges. Some of those declarations are reproduced here (from a translation in volume 2 of Miriam Lichtheim's Ancient Egyptian Literature*).*

O Wide-of-stride who comes from On: I have not done evil.

O Flame-grasper who comes from Kheraha: I have not robbed.

O Long-nosed who comes from Khbmun: I have not coveted.

O Shadow-eater who comes from the cave: I have not stolen.

O Savage-faced who comes from Rostau: I have not killed people. . . .

O Flint-eyed who comes from Khem: I have not cheated.

O Fiery-one who comes backward: I have not stolen a god's property.

O Bone-smasher who comes from Hnes: I have not told lies.

O Flame-thrower who comes from Memphis: I have not seized food.

O Cave-dweller who comes from the west: I have not sulked.

O White-toothed who comes from Lakeland: I have not trespassed. . . .

O Wanderer who comes from Bubastis: I have not spied. . . .

O Fiend who comes from the slaughterhouse: I have not committed adultery.

Osiris provided the central path to salvation in the afterlife. Here, a deceased official and his wife meet with Osiris, hoping to gain his favor.

the sun. The *bas* of countless millions traveled with Ra until he disappeared beneath earth in the west. Then each *ba* returned to its body and rested until morning, when the process began again. In another variation, the souls of the dead remained with Ra on his journey through the Duat, where he temporarily became one with Osiris.

Salvation Through Osiris

It is clear that the god Osiris played a central role in these visions of the final judgment and afterlife. In fact, his position was crucial because he provided the basic and essential context for and driving force behind human salvation and eternal existence after death. Osiris did this through a great personal sacrifice in which he suffered a cruel death and then underwent resurrection. In a sense he was a Christ-like figure. It is not surprising, therefore, that his tale was the central myth of Egyptian religion. As Richard Wilkinson puts it, the story offered

> the hope of immortality through resurrection, which had a universal appeal and was claimed at first by kings and eventually by nobles and commoners also. . . . Osiris was viewed as a benign deity who represented the clearest idea of physical salvation available to the ancient Egyptian.[48]

The essentials of this important story were that Osiris had been chosen by Ra to be pharaoh of Egypt. Aided by his wise and loving wife, Isis, Osiris proved to be a competent and fair ruler. But the king's brother, Seth, was jealous of him. Seth plotted and carried out Osiris's murder and even went so far as to cut his body into hundreds of pieces and scatter them across Egypt. However, the killer had underestimated the power of Isis's love and loyalty. She searched relentlessly until she had found every piece of her husband's body, then used magic to resurrect him. That night they conceived a son, Horus, and the next day Ra made Osiris lord of the Underworld.

The Osiris story also established the pharaoh's role in the afterlife and cycle of birth and death and provided a justification for the great power wielded by Egypt's kings. The Egyptians saw the kingship as "an essential element in the proper functioning of both the state and the cosmos," David Silverman points out. "The reigning pharaoh was the link between the gods and the world of humankind."[49]

Thus, whatever the fate of ordinary people in the afterlife, the pharaoh was thought to have a special destiny. At least by the later centuries of the Old Kingdom, the common belief was that when the king died he became one with Osiris, the model for kingship. At the same time, the new pharaoh became infused with the spirit of Osiris's son, Horus. When the new king died, he became Osiris and the next royal successor became Horus, and so it went for eternity. In this way, Osiris provided a path for all Egyptians, royal and nonroyal, to the afterlife, which was seen as part of a grand and never-ending cycle of life, death, and rebirth.

Chapter Six

Mummies and Embalming

A mong the numerous preparations that many Egyptians made in anticipation of reaching the afterlife was the process of mummification (or embalming). This traditional and time-honored death and burial ritual was seen as essential because it dehydrated and thereby preserved the body of the deceased. The widely held belief was that the corpse must be kept in the best possible condition; otherwise, it could not house the *ka* and *ba* and facilitate the dead person's journey beyond the world of the living.

The Need for Embalming

In a sense, the development of embalming in Egypt imitated nature. During the country's earliest centuries, before elaborate stone tombs began to be built, everyone buried their dead in the dry sands that were—and remain—so abundant in the country. Bodies were placed "in shallow pit graves on the edge of the desert," A. Rosalie David

explains, "and the combination of the Sun's heat and the dryness of the sand ensured that the body tissues became desiccated [thoroughly dried out] before decomposition occurred."[50] In fact, this method of burial was never abandoned in Egypt. Even in later centuries, after mummification had been perfected, most poor Egyptians could not afford to have it done. So they continued to rely on burying their dead in shallow desert graves and allowing heat, dryness, and other natural forces to do their work.

Those who could afford it began to lay their loved ones to rest in stone-lined tombs in the late Predynastic Period, perhaps around 3400 B.C. They immediately observed that the environmental conditions inside these crypts inhibited the drying process and caused rapid decomposition of bodies. In an effort to halt this natural decay, the Egyptians developed artificial embalming techniques in the centuries that followed. And by about 2500

B.C., the mummification process had become fairly sophisticated and effective.

Contrary to popular belief, the family of a deceased person did not initiate the process immediately after death. First there was a preliminary funeral, similar to a modern wake, in which people displayed and openly mourned over the body. After his trip to Egypt, Herodotus wrote:

> When a distinguished man dies, all the women of the household plaster their heads and faces with mud, then, leaving the body indoors, [walk through the streets of] the town . . . their dresses fastened with a girdle, and beat their breasts. The men . . . follow the same procedure, wearing a girdle and beating themselves like the women. The ceremony over, they take the body to be mummified.[51]

The Embalmers

The embalming process was long, complicated, laborious, and sometimes quite expensive. The cost varied according to the quality, which was essentially determined by the elaborateness of the rituals and the amount of time they took. As is true today, the family could choose between premium and lower-cost options offered by embalmers. According to Herodotus, "the best and most expensive kind" was that in which the body was carefully prepared to represent popular conceptions of what Osiris looked like at his own funeral (after Isis had restored his body). "The next best" embalming option, Herodotus said,

> is somewhat inferior and cheaper, while the third sort is the cheapest of all. After pointing out these differences in quality, [the embalmers] ask which

The mummified remains of the New Kingdom pharaoh Ramesses I (reigned ca. 1295-1294 B.C.) lie beside his sarcophagus in the Cairo Museum.

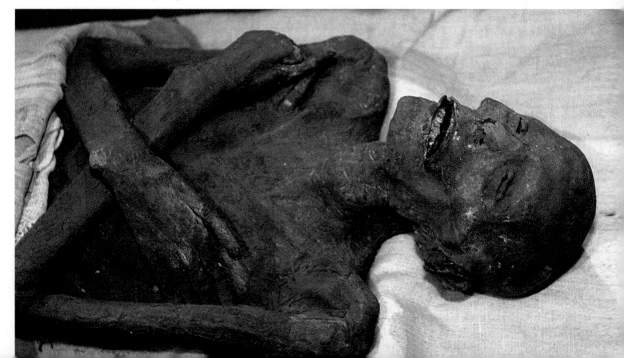

of the three is required, and the kinsmen of the dead man, having agreed upon a price, go away and leave the embalmers to do their work.[52]

"Work" is certainly a fitting word to describe the mummification process, as the embalmers' art was viewed as a distinct profession, in fact one of the most important and respected in society. Part of this prestige derived from the fact that death and burial rituals were so important in Egypt. Also, most embalmers were priests, or perhaps more accurately priest doctors. It appears that they belonged to a special class of priests for whom preparing bodies for burial was a full-time career. Often their positions were hereditary, as fathers trained their sons and the sons eventually took over the business.

The locations of the permanent embalming workshops, which the Egyptians called "places of purification," are largely unknown. But the scholarly consensus is that they were probably located near temples. They could not be too near, however, because the actual process of embalming was seen as ritually impure and might "contaminate" sacred grounds. It is fairly certain that temporary embalming facilities were sometimes set up near tombs, but again, not so close as to contaminate a tomb.

These workshops were often large-scale operations. The embalmer who ran a large shop employed numerous people, each of whom specialized in some area. Among these were coffin makers, for example. There was also a scribe who kept track of the bodies and supplies and supervised the initial embalming stage in which the body's internal organs were removed. The actual removal of the organs was done by a "cutter." His job was viewed as unclean because of the perceived high risk of contamination by evil spirits associated with such intimate contact with corpses; consequently, a cutter usually had low social status and most peo-

A Prayer Said by Embalmers

According to the third-century Greek philosopher Porphyry, Egyptian embalmers recited a prayer while removing the deceased's internal organs. This translation comes from Bob Brier's Egyptian Mummies.

Among other observances made to the corpse, they privately remove the intestines and place them in a chest . . . while one of those occupied in embalming the body recites a prayer . . . to the following effect: "O Lord Sun and all you gods that give life to men, receive me favorably and commit me to abide with the everlasting gods. For as long as I continued in that life [on earth], I have steadfastly reverenced the gods whom my parents instructed me to worship, and I have ever honored those who brought my body into the world; while as concerns my fellow men, I have done no murder, nor betrayed a trust, nor committed any other deadly sin."

ple kept their distance from him if they saw him in public. The embalmer, whose status was much higher, supervised the wrapping of the mummy. While doing so, it was customary for him to wear a mask of Anubis, god of embalming, one of many religious rituals involved in the embalming process.

Removing the Internal Organs

No substantial native Egyptian descriptions of the embalming process have survived. Two tomb paintings in Thebes show mummies being wrapped in linen, but little else; and some written text on a couple of surviving papyri describe the wrapping and a few of the religious ceremonies accompanying embalming. To learn about how mummies were actually made in ancient Egypt, modern scholars and other observers have had to rely on the accounts of two Greek historians who visited Egypt—Herodotus and Diodorus Siculus.

Both of these writers agreed that the first major step in the embalming process was the removal of the internal organs. According to Herodotus, "As much as possible of the brain is extracted through the nostrils with an iron hook, and what the hook cannot reach is rinsed out with drugs."[53] Actually, this practice varied over time. During the Old Kingdom, the brain was left inside the skull; in the ages that followed, embalmers developed the techniques Herodotus describes. Some people today are shocked to learn that the pieces of brain removed this way were usually discarded. "Apparently," Bob Brier writes,

they thought it had no important function and thus did not have to be preserved. The ancient Egyptians believed that a person thought with his heart, not his brain. In excitement it is the heart that beats quickly, not the brain. In some papyri the word for heart can also be translated as *mind*.[54]

In the next step, Herodotus recalled, "the flank [side of the body] is laid open with a flint knife and the whole contents of the abdomen removed; the cavity is then thoroughly cleaned and washed out."[55] The lungs were removed next through an incision made in the chest, but the heart, seen as the seat of intellect, was left in place. Evidence shows that sometimes various organs were removed through the rectum.

During the Old, Middle, and New kingdoms, the organs were usually dried after removal and placed in special containers called canopic jars. Mourners laid the jars near the mummy in the tomb. Beginning in the Twenty-first Dynasty, the first one following the close of the New Kingdom (ca. 1069 B.C.), it became customary to wrap the organs in small parcels and place these inside the chest or abdominal cavity. Another later variation was to wrap all the insides in one parcel and place it on the mummy's legs.

Drying and Wrapping the Body

After the removal of the organs, the embalmers put spices and other pleasant-smelling substances inside the body cavities and sewed up the incisions. Then they

This early-twentieth-century painting depicts embalmers wrapping the mummy of King Tutankhamun while a priest burns incense to please the gods.

dried out the body, a process that could take up to forty days. (The entire embalming process often took seventy days, but close to thirty of these were devoted to religious rituals.) The drying agent was natron (or natrum), a mineral salt. Herodotus wrote: "The body is placed in [a vat of] natrum [and] covered entirely over."[56]

At the end of forty days the embalmers washed the now desiccated body. Then, in Herodotus's words, they "wrapped it from head to foot in linen cut into strips and smeared on the underside with gum, which is commonly used by the Egyptians instead of glue."[57] This so-called gum or glue was actually a plant resin that dried to a rock-hard consistency and did an excellent job of keeping moisture out. Here, Herodotus seems to have gotten some of the steps in the wrong order. Examinations of a number of mummies indicate that the resin was applied to most or all of the body *before* it was wrapped in linen. The linen consisted of strips of cloth, roughly fifteen feet long on average and when possible cut from the deceased person's own bedsheets and towels.

Recital of specific prayers and magical incantations seems to have accompanied these and other steps in the embalming process. After coating the body in resin, for instance, the embalmer-priest chanted, in part:

The perfume of Arabia has been brought to you to make perfect your smell through the scent of the god [Osiris]. Here are brought to you liquids which have come from Ra to make perfect ... your smell in the Hall [of Judgment]. . . . Osiris [here a reference to both the god and the deceased, who was soon to become one with Osiris], you have received the perfume. . . . You will unite with Osiris in the great Hall. . . . You cry to

Isis, and Osiris hears your voice, and Anubis comes to you [to take you to the final judgment]. . . . Oh Osiris, may the Eye of Horus cause that which flows forth from it [beneficial magic] to come to you and to your heart forever![58]

Mummification of Animals

Today people interested in ancient Egyptian culture pay a great deal of attention to these rituals and ceremonies surrounding human mummification. Some are surprised to learn that the Egyptians also embalmed many animals. This was

Embalmers' Tools

In this excerpt from his book about ancient Egyptian life, Charles University scholar Eugen Strouhal provides the following fascinating information about the workshops and tools of ancient Egyptian embalmers.

The embalming workshops were permanent buildings of mud-brick or stone, surrounded with a high wall to shield them from unauthorized eyes. . . . The ruins of the embalming workshop at Deir el-Bahri contained several small chambers where pots and packets of natron were kept, along with vessels full of straw for stuffing the mummies, fragments of papyri, and other things. The 12th-dynasty tomb of Ipy at Deir el-Bahri contained a wooden embalming table with traces of resin and natron still on it. . . . Around it were wooden blocks, on which the body would have been placed

during mummification. . . . The embalmer's tools included a spirally curved copper hook for breaking through the . . . ethmoid bone [in the back of the nose] to remove the brain, a large flint or obsidian knife used traditionally for religious reasons to open the abdomen below the left ribs, an ordinary metal knife for cutting up the entrails [intestines], and tongs for inserting . . . stuffing through short incisions in the skin.

Tools for embalming bodies, along with jars for storing internal organs, rest in a Paris museum.

partly because a number of beasts were closely associated with gods, and some were raised and protected in temple enclosures. Not surprisingly, it was viewed as both criminal and sacrilegious to kill or harm these creatures. About the high esteem placed on such sacred animals, Herodotus said:

A mummified cat, from Egypt's Late Period, on display at the Louvre in Paris.

The various sorts have guardians appointed for them, sometimes men, sometimes women, who are responsible for feeding them; and the office of guardian is handed down from father to son. . . . Anyone who directly kills one of these animals is punished with death; should one be killed accidentally, the penalty is whatever the priests choose to impose; but for killing an ibis [a water bird] or a hawk, whether deliberately or not, the penalty is inevitably death.[59]

Cats were especially prized and venerated in Egypt. Diodorus Siculus penned an account of how, after a visiting Roman accidentally killed a cat, an angry crowd chased and killed him. And Herodotus wrote that the death of a cat "causes the Egyptians deep distress." In a household that suffered the loss of a pet cat, he said, the members of the family "shave their eyebrows"[60] as a token of respect.

Herodotus went on to say that dearly departed cats were mummified. He mentioned Bubastis (in the southeastern sector of the Nile Delta) as a center for cat embalming. The ceremonies involved invoked the powers of the local goddess Bastet, who was depicted as a cat. And there was a sacred cat cemetery at Bubastis.

Many other animals were mummified as well, including dogs, sheep, cows, jackals, birds, monkeys, snakes, mice, and even fish. In fact, they were embalmed by the millions across ancient Egypt. The four major reasons for this practice were as follows. First, many people mummified their

Why the Egyptians Honored Animals

The ancient Egyptians mummified animals because they held many of them in high esteem, seeing some as having connections with the divine. Scholar A. Rosalie David speculates about some of the reasons for this veneration in this passage from her informative handbook to ancient Egyptian life.

The reasons behind the deification of animals in ancient Egypt are not clear. Possibly some were worshiped because they assisted mankind, while others, who were feared (such as the jackals who ransacked the cemeteries), were deified in an attempt to propitiate [appease] them. It is evident, however, that animal and fetish [part-animal, part-human] forms were regarded as symbols through which the divine power could manifest itself and that animal worship continued to be extremely important through the historic period. A few of the gods, such as Ptah, the creator god of Memphis, were always represented with a full human form, but most retained some animal characteristics.

pets out of love and the desire to see them live on in the afterlife; second, some animals were embalmed so that they would survive in the afterlife as a food source for deceased humans; other animals were mummified as offerings to the gods; and finally, as Herodotus described, some were preserved through embalming because they were sacred animals.

Regarding the manner in which animals were mummified, for a long time modern scholars assumed that less time and care was taken with dead animals than with dead humans. However, this assumption was recently challenged. In 2004 a group of investigators led by Richard Evershed of the University of Bristol published the results of their chemical analysis of the tissues and wrappings of several Egyptian hawk, cat, and ibis mummies. They found that these creatures were embalmed using some of the same substances employed in human mummification. Furthermore, the same level of care that was customary for humans seems to have been given to the animals.

Not all animal mummies received such top-notch treatment, but Evershed's study suggests that at least those of sacred beasts and beloved pets did. And this speaks volumes about the compassion and humanity of the remarkable ancient inhabitants of the Nile Valley. The well-known adage that the manner in which someone treats his or her fellow humans is reflected in the way he or she treats animals was as true then as it is today.

Chapter Seven

Rituals to Honor the Dead

The embalming of bodies in preparation for burial was only a small facet of the collective array of funerary practices and rituals performed by the ancient Egyptians. Some of these rituals, of course, were designed to honor the gods. But many were meant to honor departed humans and merely invoked the blessings and/or mercy of the gods. First, there were the initial funeral ceremonies, which, on the surface, were not all that different from those performed today. Some notable differences, however, involve the Egyptians' use of certain ritual props, objects that had symbolic or magical meaning to both the living and the dead. These included sacred boats, funerary cones, and special figurines placed in the grave or tomb. The Egyptians also staged funerary games of various kinds in honor of the recently departed.

Other rituals were performed in the months and years following the official burial. These not only renewed and maintained emotional ties between the deceased

and his or her loved ones but also sought to keep evil spirits from harassing the deceased. These, as well as the initial funeral rites honoring the dead, were supported by an extensive collection of funerary texts, including spells, prayers, and religious instructions. Often rich in imagery, such writings guided both the deceased and the mourners through the inevitable transition from life to death.

Funerals and Funerary Cults

Two basic kinds of funerary ritual followed someone's death. First and foremost was the funeral proper, constituting the initial stage of mourning. As Herodotus attested, there was a wakelike ceremony in which the body rested inside the house and the relatives grieved. There might be one or more marches through the nearby streets, during which mourners beat their chests and a priest or sometimes the embalmer rapped two sticks together. (Perhaps the rapping of the sticks set the pace for the marchers.) After an unknown number of days, probably two or three, and assuming they could afford it, the mourners took the corpse to the embalmer.

After the mummification process (or instead of it if the family was poor), the mourners took part in a more elaborate funeral ceremony. It varied somewhat from one historical age to another, although the basics were always roughly the same. In the Old Kingdom, people dressed in their best clothes and marched in another mournful procession. This time they bore the body, now in a coffin, to the burial site, usually in the desert. Somewhere along the way they stopped at a shrine. There, some women, and possibly some men, too, danced in honor of the deceased. Then the spouse of the deceased and the priest-embalmer made offerings to the gods and performed a sacrifice, often slaughtering

one or more animals. Finally, the mourners carried the body to the tomb or gravesite and interred it. There is also evidence of ceremonial meals occurring at the tomb, during which it was thought that the deceased and the living shared a meal together.

A few significant changes in this routine were added later. In the Middle Kingdom, for instance, the spouse and perhaps other relatives and friends gave speeches at the shrine or tomb. Many people give speeches to honor the dead at modern funerals; these tend to be fairly informal, as they recall incidents from the deceased's life. Evidence indicates that the speeches given at ancient Egyptian funerals were more formal, consisting of traditional phrases and chants taken from major funerary texts.

In the New Kingdom, funerals became even more elaborate—for those who could afford it. Scholar Ann M. Roth provides

A modern painting shows the funeral procession of a royal or noble Egyptian. Priests carry a sacred boat in which a statue of the sun god Ra sits.

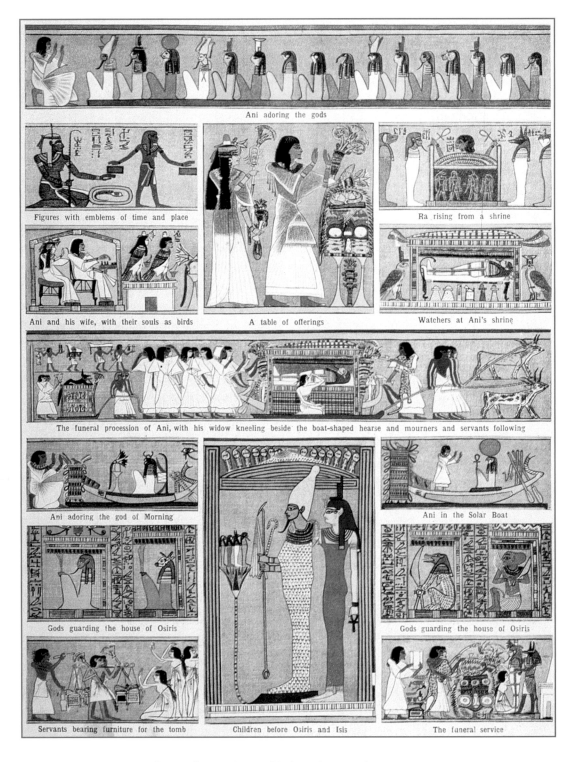

Ani adoring the gods

Figures with emblems of time and place

Ra rising from a shrine

Ani and his wife, with their souls as birds

A table of offerings

Watchers at Ani's shrine

The funeral procession of Ani, with his widow kneeling beside the boat-shaped hearse and mourners and servants following

Ani adoring the god of Morning

Ani in the Solar Boat

Gods guarding the house of Osiris

Gods guarding the house of Osiris

Servants bearing furniture for the tomb

Children before Osiris and Isis

The funeral service

68   Mummies, Myth, and Magic: Religion in Ancient Egypt

this overview based on various examples of surviving pictorial and written evidence:

> The coffin was placed on a canopied sledge [a sledlike carrier covered by canvas], often pulled by both oxen and male mourners. It was accompanied by a group of priests. . . . [The] canopic jars that held the . . . internal organs removed from the body . . . [were] placed in a small shrine that was dragged on a sledge some distance behind the coffin. . . . [Other] men carried the furniture and other grave goods of the deceased. . . . On arriving at the tomb, the mummy . . . was removed from its box coffin and set upright to receive the blessings of the rituals. . . . These included the pulling of the (empty) sarcophagus back and forth by a priest, who pulled it to the north, and an embalmer, who pulled it to the south. . . . The sarcophagus, mummy, and canopic chest were then probably introduced into the tomb, along with the funerary furniture. The ceremony closed with protective ritual recitations.[61]

The second basic kind of funerary ritual consisted of the practices and ceremonies that took place after the deceased was laid to rest. The focus of this activity was the funeral cult. Essentially, such a cult consisted of a group of people, usually including priests and relatives of the deceased. For an undetermined length of time, which might be months, years, decades, or even centuries in the case of a few famous pharaohs, these people dedicated prayers, hymns, sacrifices, and other offerings to the memory of the dead person. The funerary cults of the pharaohs were the largest and most conspicuous; entire mortuary temples were erected to house them. Funerary cults dedicated to ordinary people were much less elaborate. And poor people could not afford them at all.

Funerary Boats, Cones, and Figurines

Regardless of the variations in rituals, throughout Egypt's ancient history funeral ceremonies used objects that had special symbolic or magical meaning. Among the more important and visibly obvious of these props were boats that bore bodies and coffins. The idea of the sacred boat was derived from early myths and artistic representations of the gods traveling in boats. The most famous example was that of the sun god, Ra, who rode in a ship as he made his daily journey across the sky.

Accordingly, sacred boats became regular fixtures in the processions held at religious festivals. David Silverman describes the use of such vessels at the Opet Festival, in which priests carried the images of Amun-Ra and other deities from Karnak to Luxor:

> As the procession of priests slowly carried the ceremonial boats to the water's

A copy of the Book of the Dead displays images of common Egyptian death rituals.

edge, singers, dancers, acrobats, musicians, military men, and local residents would have swarmed around the procession. At the bank of the Nile, the processional [boats] were placed on river-going boats, the greatest being the "Mighty of Prow," which carried the [boat] of Amun.... The ram head of Amun, draped with necklaces ... decorated the bow and stern posts.... Once the statue of the god was loaded ... the boat was drawn southward, against the current, by gangs of sailors heaving on tow ropes.[62]

Partly in imitation of such festival ceremonies honoring the gods, mourners employed boats in funeral ceremonies honoring the dead. The mummy and/or coffin was usually placed in a ceremonial boat, for instance, and the pallbearers carried or dragged the boat during the funeral procession. When possible, the ceremonial boat was placed aboard a real boat on the Nile for a short but religiously meaningful trip mimicking the ship journeys of the gods.

Another conspicuous prop associated with funerals was the funerary cone. It seems to have been introduced in the early Middle Kingdom, but its height of popularity was in the New Kingdom. Such cones were small objects (generally five or six inches high) made of baked clay. People often placed groups of them above the door at the entrances of tombs, sometimes as many as two or three hundred at a time. Each cone contained written words, including the dead person's name, the names of relatives, and sometimes a short message. Scholars are not sure about the purpose of these objects, and numerous theories have been proposed to explain them. One is that they marked the boundary of the tomb;

Funeral barges bear the coffin and some of the grave goods of a deceased king along the Nile. Boats were a common motif of Egyptian funerals.

another suggests they were symbolic of the solar disk sacred to the god Ra.

Still another common object associated with the dead and funerary rites was a figurine called a *shawabti* (or *shabti*). It was common to see several in each tomb or grave. The Egyptians believed that these small statues would magically spring to life and perform menial labor for the deceased person in the afterlife. Because daily life revolved mainly around agriculture, Bob Brier explains, people

> viewed the next world also as primarily agrarian. They believed that the deceased would have to plant the fields and maintain irrigation canals, so the little statues buried in tombs began to look more like field workers than mummies. They retained the mummiform shape so as to be identified with Osiris . . . but their hands were shown protruding from the bandages so as to be able to do work.[63]

Each *shawabti* was marked with the name of the deceased and also with a spell intended to force the figurine to work for the deceased. The following example from the New Kingdom was found in the grave of a workman named Setau:

> Setau, justified, says: Oh, this *shawabti!* . . . If one reckons Setau, justified, to do any work which is done there [in the afterlife]—now indeed an obligation has been set up for him there . . . to cultivate the fields. . . . If you [the *shawabti*] are called at any

Exorcizing Evil Ghosts

Most Egyptian death rituals dealt with benevolent spirits, such as the souls, or ghosts, of dearly departed loved ones. But the Egyptians believed in evil spirits, too. One common belief was that bad spirits could harass or terrorize the living and cause people to become sick or even die from disease. Clearly, such malign ghosts had to be exorcized (destroyed or driven away). One way to do this was to break in to the tomb in which the spirit's body was interred and damage or burn the mummy and/or the figurines or paintings of the person. It was thought that this might threaten the ghost's very existence in the Underworld. Another approach was to use other spirits residing in the afterlife against the evil ones. It was fairly common, for example, to seek out old graves that no one visited anymore, believing that those buried in them had become angry over being neglected. People placed offerings in these graves in hopes of persuading the disgruntled spirits to attack the evil ghosts in the hereafter.

time [to do such work], "Here I am!" you shall say.[64]

Funerary Texts

Also frequently found in tombs and graves were varying quantities of funerary texts. Consisting mainly of collected spells and chants related to death and the afterlife, these texts were seen to possess wisdom and, if applied properly, potent magical powers. The earliest surviving versions are the so-called Pyramid Texts. The name comes from the fact that they were found carved onto the interior walls of some pyramid tombs of the late Old Kingdom. Notable, for example, are those from the pyramid of the pharaoh Unas (reigned ca. 2375–2345 B.C.). These and other examples from the period provide a great deal of information about the proper ways for royalty to reach and thrive in the afterlife.

Another series of funerary texts appeared between about 2040 and 1780 B.C. Modern scholars dubbed them the Coffin Texts because they were painted onto the caskets of Egyptian nobles, as well as written on papyri in private tombs. To a large extent, the Coffin Texts were an edited version of the Pyramid Texts. What made the later versions different was their application to the burial and salvation of ordinary people. "They are often said to reflect the democratization of the afterlife," noted Egyptologist Ian Shaw points out, "whereby individuals were no longer dependent on the ruler for their afterlife."[65] Notable among the Coffin Texts are sayings intended as guides to direct the deceased in his or her journeys in the next life.

In the years following the era in which the Coffin Texts appeared, the guidebook function of funerary writings increased in importance and reached its most fully developed form in the Book of the Dead, introduced shortly before the start of the New Kingdom. About half of the spells and chants in the book were derived from the Pyramid and Coffin texts. The most famous part of the Book of the Dead is chapter 125, which describes the final judgment before Osiris and contains the text of the negative confession. Part of chapter 6 became a formula widely used in work orders inscribed on *shawabtis*. Another popular spell, from chapter 109, was intended to be recited by the deceased to gain entrance onto Ra's sacred sky boat. Part of it reads:

I know that northern gate of the sky . . . the place where Ra navigates by the winds and by the oar. I am in charge of the rigging in the god's ship. I am a tireless oarsman in the bark [boat] of Ra. I know those twin sycamores of turquoise between which Ra comes forth.[66]

Ritualistic Funeral Games

Cones, worker statues, and sacred texts were among the many objects that were crucial components of funerary ritual in ancient Egypt. A more active form of ritual (along with marching in processions and performing sacrifices) consisted of games and sports played at funerals in honor of the dead. Such ritual games were fairly common in the ancient world. Probably the most famous are those held in honor of a fallen warrior in the finale of the *Iliad*, the great epic poem by the eighth-century-B.C Greek bard Homer.

As did the ceremonies described in the *Iliad*, Egyptian funeral games sometimes included such events as wrestling and boxing. Scenes showing matches decorate the walls of the tomb of Kheruef, steward of Queen Tiy, the wife of the New Kingdom pharaoh Amenhotep III. Silverman describes an impressive set of paintings found in the tomb:

Six pairs of men, their heads shaved in the manner of priests, engage in what their postures and the [written] caption designate as a boxing match. However, the caption close to one boxer in each pair proclaims, "Horus has prevailed in truth!", suggesting that this man is taking the part of the god Horus (with whom the living king was identified) in a re-enactment of the battle between the forces of good and evil personified . . . by Horus and his brother Seth. As is to be expected in a ritual scene, the outcome of the boxing match is never in doubt. Horus must always triumph

King Tut's *Shawabtis*

A great many *shawabtis* (or *shabtis*), the small statues representing laborers in the afterlife, have been found by archaeologists in Egyptian tombs. The tomb of the pharaoh Tutankhamun ("King Tut"), excavated by Howard Carter beginning in 1922, had 413 of them. This total included one worker for each day of the year (365), plus 36 overseers (roughly one for every ten workers) and 12 high overseers (one for each month of the year). The inclusion of overseer *shawabtis* was based on the belief that the ordi-nary laborer *shawabtis* might become unruly and need to be disciplined. Most of these figurines were marked with the boy king's name so that it would be understood that they would work for him, not someone else, in the afterlife.

Pictured are some of the shawabtis *found in the tomb of "King Tut."*

Ptolemaic Ritual Games

Among the ritual games enacted to honor the dead in ancient Egypt were those held by the members of the royal Ptolemaic Dynasty, founded by Alexander the Great's general, Ptolemy. These rulers sponsored a major religious festival, known as the Ptolemaia, every four years. It was intended to honor those Ptolemies who had already passed on, as well as the major Egyptian gods, with whom the Ptolemies claimed a direct link.

The large-scale procession that opened the festival featured big, colorful images of both gods and Ptolemaic rulers, past and present. The athletic games staged at the festival were similar in many ways to the Olympic Games held in southern Greece every four years. The events included running, jumping, wrestling, and chariot racing, among others. The Ptolemaic games were staged not only in Egypt but also in other eastern Mediterranean regions where the Ptolemies maintained territory or influence.

over Seth, in accordance with the myth.[67]

Thus, the contest was not a true sporting event but, rather, a ritual reenactment of a myth—a sort of religious pageant—in which the priest playing Seth pretended to lose the battle at the appropriate moment.

Other sporting events besides boxing and wrestling were adopted for funerary rituals. One very popular one was stick fighting, in which the combatants represented Horus, Seth, or other gods. Also, a certain amount of religious symbolism spilled over from these games into some of the games played mainly for fun. For example, wall paintings show pharaohs playing a game in which a ball was hit by a bat; the ball apparently represented the eye of an evil serpent and the bat the power of Ra to drive the serpent away. Some board games also had religious themes, including one called "Passing Through the Underworld." These and other ritualistic games demonstrate the remarkable degree to which religion and death rituals permeated every niche of Egyptian life.

Chapter Eight

Tombs and Grave Goods

Much has been written or said about Egyptian tombs in recent years in the press, books, television, movies, and on the Internet. Indeed, thanks to some spectacular archaeological finds, in the past two centuries Egyptian tombs have captured the public imagination worldwide. This attention and publicity has made tombs and their contents (including mummies) perhaps the most recognizable aspects of Egyptian religion.

Different Tombs

The widespread attention accorded to these tombs has also given some people the impression that all ancient Egyptians were buried in tombs made of stone or bricks. However, the majority of people in ancient Egypt could not afford formal tombs. Throughout most of that country's history, the average poor family wrapped the body of a loved one in a shroud of linen or reeds and buried it in a makeshift grave in the sand.

For those families that could afford tombs, whether grand or humble, after a body was embalmed the funeral procession bore it to the burial site, where a brick or stone tomb had been prepared. Such crypts varied widely in type, shape, and size. The largest and most famous are the pyramids, dozens of which have survived in various states of preservation. The biggest and most awe-inspiring pyramids are the three giants that rest on the Giza plateau on the outskirts of modern Cairo. These and other pyramids were the final resting places of pharaohs and their kin. Later, a number of pharaohs were interred in tombs that were hewn, or cut, out of solid mountain rock.

Numerous smaller stone, brick, or rock-hewn tombs—some built for the nobility, others for ordinary people—have been found in the Nile Valley. Several noble tombs came to light in the 1800s and early 1900s; one of the most notable was that of a well-to-do architect named Kha, uncovered in

The tombs and houses of workers at Deir el Medina, near ancient Thebes, show archaeologists how ordinary Egyptians lived and buried their dead.

1906. Few tombs of Egyptians of average means were found before the late twentieth century, however. One of the most important finds in this regard occurred in the 1990s, when renowned archaeologists Mark Lehner and Zahi Hawass began excavating an ancient workers' village located on the Giza plateau near the pyramids. They found a workers' cemetery containing more than six hundred humble tombs. Most of these consist of pits dug in the sand and then lined with mud bricks and crowned by stone caps measuring between two and six feet across.

Whether built for rich, privileged people or poorer workers, all Egyptian tombs had certain things in common. In particular, all originally contained varying quantities of grave goods. These goods included food, clothes, tools, weapons, and other items to help the deceased sustain him- or herself in the tomb and afterlife.

From Mastabas to Pyramids

Not surprisingly, the first substantial tombs in Egypt, which were made of sun-dried mud bricks, were constructed to house the bodies of kings and other members of the upper classes. These tombs first appeared about 3400 B.C. and continued to be built for many centuries afterward. They were called mastabas. The name came from an Egyptian word meaning "bench" because they were flat-topped rectangular structures that looked something like the simple wooden benches that many Egyptians placed near the front doors of their homes.

Each mastaba had several chambers, including the all-important burial chamber, which housed the body of the deceased. The mastaba of the First Dynasty pharaoh Aha (reigned ca. 3100 B.C.), for example, had five chambers, of which the one in the center contained his body. This early form of burial chamber "was reached by means of a shaft that led down from the roof of the *mastaba*," A. Rosalie David explains.

In the earliest examples, the interior walls were lined with matting or strengthened with wooden planks, but in early dynastic times [beginning in Aha's era] this developed into a wooden coffin or a wood-paneled chamber. The wooden coffin (which eventually entirely replaced the custom of placing the body in a reed mat) was placed in a recess cut into the side and floor of the burial pit.[68]

Over time, the Egyptians found to their dismay that mastabas had two serious shortcomings. First, the mud bricks with which they were built disintegrated relatively rapidly, so these tombs were not permanent. Second, even when mud bricks are new they are far softer than stone and fairly easy to cut into or demolish using stone or metal tools; this made mastabas the frequent target of tomb robbers.

Hoping to increase the permanence and security of the bench tombs, the Egyptians eventually began using stone for large portions of the superstructure. This improvement in turn led to the development of a new and larger kind of tomb. In preparing the tomb of the second pharaoh of the Old Kingdom, Djoser (2667–2648 B.C.), the architect Imhotep (who would later become an Egyptian icon and be worshipped as a god) originally planned for a large stone mastaba.

The famous stepped pyramid of the Old Kingdom pharaoh Djoser was designed by the architect Imhotep. When first erected it was about two hundred feet tall.

At some point, however, he concocted a novel idea. He ended up stacking six stone mastabas on top of one another, each slightly smaller than the one beneath it, thereby creating the world's first pyramid tomb. Each succeeding level is recessed inward several feet from the one below it, creating a notched effect. This gives the appearance of a series of big steps, hence its nickname the "Step Pyramid." The structure originally measured 413 feet long and 344 feet wide at its base and towered some 200 feet high.

The Age of Pyramids

In the twentieth century, the United States and other major nations engaged in an arms race, each attempting to build bigger and more lethal weapons than the others. Similarly, the Egyptian pharaohs who followed Djoser got into what might be termed a "pyramid race," in which each tried to match or surpass the tombs erected by his predecessors. This initiated what the modern world looks back on as the great age of pyramid building. Most of these structures were erected in a roughly nine-century span beginning just after 2700 B.C. and ending shortly after 1800 B.C.

At first, royal architects merely copied Imhotep's design and built step pyramids. But soon an important development occurred. The builders filled in the notches, or steps, creating the first smooth-sided pyramids. For example, the great pyramid at Meidum, situated several miles south of Giza, was originally a step pyramid built for King Huni or perhaps his son, King Sneferu; but a later pharaoh transformed it into a smooth-sided pyramid. Subsequently, other pyramids were designed as smooth-sided from the outset.

The most imposing of these "true" pyramids were those at Giza. The three enormous edifices were erected in a period of only about seventy-five years (ca. 2585–ca. 2510 B.C.) by the pharaohs Khufu, Khafre, and Menkaure. The largest of the group, that of Khufu, originally stood 481 feet high and its base covered more than thirteen acres. Khafre's pyramid was a close second at a height of 478 feet, and Menkaure's tomb was 220 feet high.

Large stone pyramids were very time-consuming to build and relied on an inordinate amount of human and material resources. For example, Khufu's tomb kept at least ten thousand people busy for a generation and required up to 2.3 million blocks of stone, each weighing several tons. In short, pyramids were hugely expensive endeavors. Over time, therefore, their size decreased and fewer were built. The pharaohs largely abandoned pyramid tombs by the end of the Middle Kingdom. The last one erected in Egypt was probably that of Ahmose (reigned ca. 1550–1525 B.C.), which was only thirty to forty feet high.

Rediscovering the Hidden Tombs

Another reason that the Egyptian government gave up on building pyramids was that these structures were too accessible to tomb robbers. No matter how big, sturdy, and well guarded, all pyramids fell prey to thieves within a few centuries at most. The

The renowned pyramids of Khufu, Khafre, and Menkaure, at Giza, near modern Cairo, were the largest tombs ever built by the ancient Egyptians.

pharaohs eventually realized that they needed less conspicuous tombs that would be more difficult for the robbers to find and exploit. To this end, the rulers of the New Kingdom carved their tombs from solid rock mountainsides. Most are in the so-called Valley of the Kings, a remote, rugged, very bleak area near the west bank of the Nile near Thebes. Each tomb had a small entrance that was purposely hidden after the tomb was sealed. Inside were varying numbers of mostly small, rock-walled chambers, each leading to one or more others.

Unfortunately for the pharaohs, the tomb robbers were extremely clever and persistent and eventually managed to despoil the treasures hidden in the Valley of the Kings. In fact, all across Egypt the graves of monarchs, nobles, and others were pillaged, stripped of most or all of their con-

tents, and left to be buried by shifting sands and forgotten. Thus, millennia later, when modern archaeologists began rediscovering the wonders of ancient Egypt, they found very few undisturbed tombs.

Still, even the empty tombs revealed much about how they were constructed. And the handful that remained largely intact seemed that much more special and exciting. Although excavations remain ongoing, most of the important ancient Egyptian tombs were uncovered in the first half of the twentieth century, which is often referred to as the "golden age" of Egyptology.

One of the more spectacular finds was the tomb of Kha, architect of Amenhotep III and at least two of his predecessors. This tomb, one of the few the tomb robbers had overlooked, was uncovered at Thebes in 1906 by Italian excavator Ernesto Schiaparelli.

Tombs and Grave Goods 79

A Spectacular Royal Tomb Recently Unearthed

The discovery of spectacular ancient Egyptian tombs did not end with the famous unearthing of King Tut's final resting place in 1922. In 1985 American Egyptologist Kent R. Weeks discovered an extraordinary Egyptian royal tomb in the Valley of the Kings, near the site of ancient Thebes. (Actually, another digger, James Burton, had found the tomb in 1825, but sand and other debris later covered its entrance and it was lost.) Dubbed KV5 by archaeologists, the crypt, built for the more than fifty sons of the pharaoh Ramesses II, contains a complex of more than one hundred chambers, all linked by corridors. A great deal of burial equipment such as coffins, canopic jars, *shawabtis*, and grave goods like chariots, jewelry, vases, and clothing have been found in the labyrinthian tomb. According to Weeks, the work of clearing and examining all the chambers will take at least another generation.

Amazingly, everything inside lay exactly as it had been when Kha was buried some thirty-three centuries before. The men even found a tiny pile of ash residue from the oil lamp used by the person who sealed the tomb. An official observer who entered the tomb with Schiaparelli later said:

> One asked oneself in bewilderment whether the ashes here . . . had truly ceased to glow at a time when Greece and Rome were undreamed of, when Assyria did not exist, and when the Exodus of the Children of Israel was yet unaccomplished.[69]

Other ancient Egyptian tombs revealed themselves in the years that followed. In 1939 French excavator Pierre Montet found several underground chambers at Tanis in the Nile Delta, a burial complex containing the mummies of three rulers of the Twenty-first and Twenty-second dynas-ties (ca. 1070–715 B.C.). Like Kha's tomb, these burial sites had not been plundered by thieves and the contents were intact.

Though these discoveries were unusual and exciting and taught modern scholars much about Egyptian tombs, they paled in comparison to the most famous rediscovered tomb of all. In 1922, after several years of digging in the Valley of the Kings, English archaeologist Howard Carter unearthed the tomb of the pharaoh Tutankhamun, who soon came to be called "King Tut" for short. This New Kingdom ruler, who reigned from approximately 1336 to 1327 B.C., achieved little of any note and died young; yet thanks to the publicity generated from the discovery of his tomb, he has become perhaps the most famous of all ancient Egyptians. Carter found that Tut's tomb had been entered by thieves. Fortunately, though, something had scared them away before they could steal much, and almost all of the tomb's contents remained intact.

Goods to Sustain the Dead

In both number and splendor, the contents of Tut's tomb greatly surpassed any found before or since in an ancient Egyptian burial site. Together with what was found in Kha's tomb and a few others, these artifacts have revealed to the modern world the types of grave goods that the Egyptians considered essential to sustain a deceased person in the afterlife. Perhaps not surprisingly, these items are, for the most part, the same as those that ancient Egyptians used on a routine basis in their everyday lives—food, furniture, clothes, and so forth.

The contents of Kha's tomb are a case in point. Egyptologist Nicholas Reeves gives this partial list:

A series of low [wooden and woven reed] tables was piled high with offerings of vegetables, mashed carob, and loaves [of bread] in a bewildering range of sizes and shapes, while [large jars] contained fine wine, grapes, salted meats . . . and flour. . . . Next to the coffins [of Kha and his wife, Meryet,] were . . . several additional items of furniture: Meryet's bed, made up ready for use, the lady's wig, cosmetic and trinket boxes, her workbasket with needles, a razor, pins, and a comb, as well as decorated storage chests packed with clothing.[70]

The same type of functional items were found in Tut's tomb as well, only in greater numbers. The list Carter compiled included 6 chairs, 12 stools, 6 beds, 69 storage chests and boxes, and numerous clothing items, among them tunics, shirts, kilts,

The splendor of Tutankhamun's tomb is evident from this photo of his burial chamber. Hundreds of grave goods of all kinds were found in the tomb.

The remains of food from a tomb (top); and a box of vases from Kha's tomb.

caps, and gloves. The food items included bread, poultry, beef, spices, fruits, nuts, honey, and wine. (Actually, the wine itself had long ago evaporated, so the jars were empty when Carter and his assistants opened them.)

The grave goods in Egyptian tombs also included items that reflected the deceased's rank, profession, or personal interests. In Kha's tomb, for instance, archaeologists found measuring sticks and other tools used by ancient architects. Similarly, Tut's tomb contained various artifacts associated with royalty, including a throne and the crook and flail held by pharaohs during certain ceremonies. Tut's crypt also contained a large number of hunting and sporting items. Among these were 46 bows, 427 arrows, 2 bronze swords, 2 gold daggers, 8 shields, 2 slings (for hunting birds and other small game), and 6 full-sized chariots. This reveals that Tut greatly enjoyed hunting and other outdoor activities. Several musical instruments were also found in his tomb, which suggests either that he enjoyed music or that music was important in the lives of pharaohs (or perhaps both).

Kha's architectural tools and Tut's hunting equipment and musical items reveal something of the interests and personalities of these long-dead people. But what about their physical appearance? Apparently it was customary to include paintings, masks, statues, and other representations of the deceased in the grave goods. A mask of Kha's wife was found in her coffin, for example. And the tomb contained a small wooden statue of Kha. In a like manner,

A Royal Tomb Restored

One of the largest and most splendid of the royal tombs in the Valley of the Kings was that of Ramesses VI, who reigned from circa 1143 to 1136 B.C. during the New Kingdom's declining years. Due to the destruction wrought by tomb robbers and natural forces over the years, the tomb had seriously deteriorated over the centuries. The Egyptian government recently renovated and restored it, however. For the modest sum of $3, visitors can follow a wooden walkway that leads down a corridor some 330 feet long, which was cut from the solid rock of the mountainside by ancient workers. Carefully restored paintings and hieroglyphics adorn the corridor's walls. Inside the burial chamber rests Ramesses' stone sarcophagus, which the restorers pieced back together from more than 250 fragments left by the tomb robbers' rampage. However, the facial section is an exact replica, for the real stone face now rests in the British Museum in London.

The beautifully restored tomb of the pharaoh Ramesses VI attracts thousands of visitors each year.

Tut's tomb featured a small shrine decorated with a painting of the young pharaoh, several wooden figurines depicting him, and a magnificent gold funerary mask inside his coffin. Studded with semi-precious stones, including quartz, lapis lazuli, and turquoise, the mask is an idealized, though probably fairly accurate, reproduction of the young man's face.

None of the grave goods mentioned are particularly surprising considering the importance the ancient Egyptians placed on sustaining themselves in the next world. Food, clothing, furniture, tools, leisure items, and a visual means of identifying the individual from other dead persons were all important. Sometimes, however, archaeologists find things they did not expect in the tombs. In Tut's burial chamber, for instance, Carter found two mummified infants. To this day, no one knows who they were, since the meager historical records make no mention of Tut having any children. What is more certain is that they add considerably to the universal air of mystery surrounding ancient Egyptian tombs and grave goods and the unflagging public fascination with them.

Chapter Nine

TOMB ROBBERS VIOLATE THE DEAD

Once a tomb was sealed, the vast majority of ancient Egyptians deemed it and its contents to be sacred and untouchable. To tamper with the body, the canopic jars, or the images and other grave goods of the deceased amounted to sacrilege, a severe violation of accepted religious beliefs and taboos. Stealing the food offerings might cause the deceased to starve in the afterlife; taking his or her personal items might cause the deceased extreme discomfort and despair; and worst of all, dislodging, removing, or damaging the corpse might prevent the *ka* and *ba* from fulfilling their destinies in the world beyond.

Because the act of robbing a tomb was seen to desecrate the ancient and cherished religious beliefs of the nation, people viewed it as a crime as heinous as murder or treason. Not surprisingly, someone found guilty of tomb robbing faced certain execution. Yet despite the religious, social, and legal sanctions against tomb robbing, it flourished in Egypt throughout ancient times. And nearly all of the country's richer burial sites were looted by the late fifth and early sixth centuries A.D.

The success of the tomb robbers is all the more remarkable when one considers that the government often did its best to try to stop them. It is unknown when royal and upper-class Egyptian burials became rich enough to attract thieves. It may have been as early as 3400 B.C., when brick mastabas began to be built. Certainly by the start of the First Dynasty (ca. 3100 B.C.), the government recognized that it had to find some way to protect the graves of the nation's leaders. Thereafter, increasingly elaborate and costly security methods were invented and deployed, including the most costly of all—those for the larger pyramids. Unfortunately for the authorities, and of course the families of the deceased, the tomb robbers always managed to keep pace with and circumvent new security measures. "From an early period," Dieter Arnold, an expert on these measures, writes, a contest began between builders and robbers. As soon as the architects had devised an apparently safe tomb construction, the tomb robbers learned how to surmount [overcome] the obstacle, thus forcing the architects to increase their efforts.[71]

Attempts to Block Tomb Doors

The contest between builders and robbers affected the design and integrity of all kinds of brick, stone, and rock-hewn tombs. Because of their formidable size and cost, pyramids had perhaps the most elaborate security measures, although some of the same methods used to protect their burial chambers were used in other kinds of tombs as well. In fact, one of the reasons that these large structures evolved was the need to discourage thieves. The architects and builders who raised the great pyramids at Giza, for example, installed some rather formidable safeguards. And they apparently were confident that these measures would be sufficient to keep the pillagers out.

At least six or seven different kinds of security measures evolved to secure the inner sanctums of pyramidal and other types of tombs during the Old and Middle kingdoms. The simplest was to push big, very heavy chunks of rock up against the tomb's door. This was fairly easily accomplished by a number of workers using wooden

Intruders climb through one of the main passages inside the great pyramid of Khufu.

levers and ropes. The problem, of course, was that this measure could be undone almost as easily by thieves employing levers and ropes, a fact that became obvious during the Old Kingdom. Nevertheless, this rudimentary method continued to be used for many tombs during the Middle and New kingdoms.

A more elaborate method for blocking the door of a tomb was to install one or more stone portcullises, large slabs that slid down from storage cavities above the entrance. Workers lowered them immediately after the tomb was sealed by priests and government officials. Once in place, the sides of the slab extended into grooves cut in the stone to the right and left of the door. This held the slab tightly in place and it could not be pulled or levered away. The builders of Khufu's pyramid at Giza

The Collective Tomb at Deir el-Bahri

The tomb containing more than forty royal mummies at Deir el-Bahri was originally found by a local Egyptian farmer when one of his goats fell into a deep shaft leading to the crypt. For a while, the family kept the discovery secret and sold various grave goods found inside on the black market. Eventually the authorities found out, and in July 1881 German Egyptologist Emile Brugsch began official exploration and preservation of the tomb. Brugsch later described his first reactions to seeing its contents, as quoted in a May 1887 article in Century Magazine.

Collecting my senses, I made the best examination of [the coffins] I could by the light of my torch, and at once saw that they contained the mummies of royal personages of both sexes; and yet that was not all. Plunging on ahead . . . I came to the [end] chamber . . . and there standing against the walls or here lying on the floor, I found even a greater number of mummy-cases of stupendous size and weight. Their gold coverings and polished surfaces so plainly reflected my own excited [face] that it seemed as though I was looking into the faces of my own ancestors.

This is how the royal mummies in the Deir el-Bahri tomb looked when they were found.

installed three huge portcullises, one in front of the other, outside the entrance to the inner burial chamber, which was located in the heart of the structure. Modern Egyptian tour guides regularly show visitors where these slabs once rested and explain how they were lowered into place.

Later, perhaps in the Middle Kingdom, a variation of the portcullis developed. It consisted of one or more big slabs that slid into place from the sides of the entranceway instead of from above it. The advantage of this method over the portcullis was that larger and heavier blocks could be employed, since the heavier the block, the harder it was to raise into position as a portcullis. A surviving example of the horizontal sliding block method can be seen in the pyramid of Amenemhat II (reigned ca. 1922–1878 B.C.) at Dashur, a few miles south of Memphis.

Though seemingly extremely formidable, portcullises and sliding blocks did not stop all the tomb robbers. Usually, the thieves were unable to move the slabs. But if there were no guards to stop them, they took their time and methodically chiseled through the blocks, creating a hole big enough for a person to crawl through. Another method used by the robbers was to avoid the stone slabs altogether and tunnel around them through softer materials, especially in brick structures.

Blocking Passages

Larger tombs, like the pyramids, were composed of huge amounts of stone and it was therefore very difficult and time-consuming

Tomb Portcullis

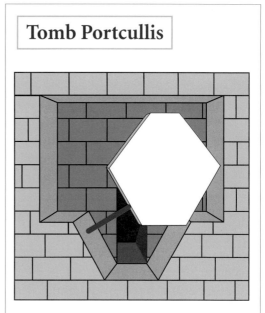

During construction, a stone portcullis was propped above an entrance.

When the building was complete, the prop was removed and the portcullis slipped into place, sealing the chamber.

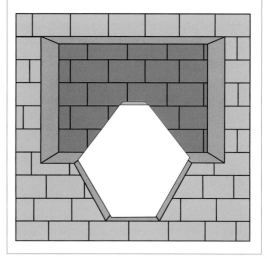

for thieves to tunnel through them. Still, the builders knew that if robbers could reach the burial chamber, its entrance might be breached even when portcullises or sliding doors were in place. An even more complex and costly security measure evolved to address this problem. It consisted of filling the entire passageway leading to the burial chamber with stone. This method was used to back up the portcullises in Khufu's pyramid. Today visitors there enjoy climbing through the so-called Grand Gallery, an impressive passageway 153 feet long and 28 feet high leading to the pharaoh's inner chamber. But for a long time after Khufu's burial, the Grand Gallery was blocked by immense quantities of stone.

Because these stone blocks no longer exist, it was at first difficult for modern investigators to ascertain how they were installed. But a number of clues discovered in Khufu's structure, as well as in other pyramids, shed some important light on the process. Arnold explains how it was applied to the Bent Pyramid (of the pharaoh Sneferu, Khufu's father) at Dashur, erected shortly before Khufu's great monument:

> In the ascending part of the passage we find for the first time a system that was later used in much grander style in the [Khufu] pyramid. Four granite plugs were built in during the construction of the passage, but kept in the uppermost part of the passage. This passage had a raised ceiling so that the traffic over the plugs during the construction and the burial were

not hindered. The plugs were temporarily kept in position by a system of wooden beams, which . . . has left its traces in the floor and side walls. These beams could be removed from below in order to release the plugs, which by their own weight would slide down into their final position without trapping the workers who carried out the maneuver.[72]

This method of plugging passages with solid stone must have seemed foolproof. And accordingly, it was used in a number of later pyramids, as well as in some smaller private tombs. However, tomb robbers were eventually able to defeat these obstacles by chiseling through them, tunneling around them, or finding narrow secret passages used as a means of escape by the workers who had installed the plugs.

Other Security Measures

Portcullises, sliding doors, and plugged passageways were all designed to protect the entrance of a burial chamber. Because thieves were able to get around these measures, some architects and builders tried a more extreme approach—eliminating the entrance altogether. This was accomplished by sealing the chamber while the tomb was under construction rather than after it was completed. Partway through the building process the burial chamber was fashioned without any doors but with an opening left in the ceiling. The body of the deceased, along with the grave goods, was lowered down through the hole. And afterward the

This burial chamber inside one of the Giza pyramids was encased in solid stone. Yet tomb robbers were still able to get inside and rob the royal treasures.

builders completed the rest of the structure, thereby encasing the chamber in solid stone.

One advantage of an encased burial chamber was secrecy. Theoretically, once the tomb was finished, potential thieves might be thwarted because they did not know where the chamber was located. This was certainly part of the strategy employed in the big pyramids at Giza, in which the royal crypts were located deep inside the structures. Adding to the air of secrecy was another line of defense consisting of the layer of casing stones that originally covered the outsides of these pyramids. After a pyramid was sealed, the last casing stone was put into place, and it blended visually

with the other casing blocks. The builders hoped that the exact location of the outer entrance would be forgotten over time, making it too difficult for thieves to know where to begin digging. However, the reality was that the location of the outer entrance was not forgotten. Numerous workers knew where it was, and over time this information passed from generation to generation.

Another extreme and very costly and time-consuming security plan utilized a resource that Egypt had in abundance—sand. The builders excavated a deep shaft in bedrock or a mountainside and created a burial chamber at the bottom. Then they filled in the shaft with thousands of tons

Using Sand to Defeat Tomb Robbers

During the Twenty-sixth Dynasty (ca. 664–525 B.C.), often referred to as the Saite period of Egyptian history, builders introduced the security method of using sand to fill in the shafts leading to royal crypts. Scholar Dieter Arnold explains how this was done in an excerpt from his book on building methods in ancient Egypt.

The major device to flood the sarcophagus [with sand] was the following. During the construction, round holes were cut into the stone vaults covering the sarcophagus. These holes were temporarily blocked with jars. . . . At the moment of closing the tomb, the bottoms of the jars were smashed and the sand streamed in, thus covering the sarcophagus. It would continue to do so if the robbers started to dig a tunnel. . . . Clever tomb robbers could have avoided the sand by digging their tunnels through the bedrock and attacking the sarcophagus from below. To prevent this possibility, some tomb builders carved a cave below the sarcophagus and connected it with the sand fill on top by vertical shafts so that this part of the cave also would be filled with sand streaming down from above.

of sand, which would be extremely time-consuming and difficult for thieves to remove.

The Time Factor

In fact, time proved to be the most crucial factor in the seemingly never-ending contest between the tomb builders and tomb robbers. It was probably clear to all involved that, given sufficient time, looters could get around any security measure the builders could devise. That is why guards were posted outside the major tombs after they were sealed. Portcullises, plugged passages, casing stones, sand pits, and other measures could be expected to work fairly well as long as the presence of the guards prevented thieves from having enough time to subvert the safeguards.

But in the long run time worked against the government and for the tomb robbers. First, posting guards at every rich tomb for twenty-four hours a day, seven days a week proved very costly and required a considerable level of commitment and vigilance over the course of years and in some cases many generations. Such a security system could remain in place and be efficient only when the country was stable and the central government reasonably strong and in control. During most of the Old, Middle, and New kingdoms, this was the case.

However, Egypt also endured several periods in which the country was less stable, more chaotic, and had a weak, divided, or decentralized government. Not long after 2200 B.C., for instance, the Old Kingdom ended and the First Intermediate Period (ca. 2181–2055 B.C.) ensued. This era witnessed political instability, disunity, power struggles, and a shifting seat of government, all of which surely disrupted and in some cases halted efforts to guard many of the richer tombs. It was probably during these troubled years that the Giza pyramids were pillaged.

Conditions improved with the onset of the Middle Kingdom. But more vandalism and looting of tombs likely occurred during the Second Intermediate Period (ca. 1650–1550 B.C.). During these years a foreign people, the Hyksos, occupied the northern region of the country. And the native Egyptian government, which ruled the south from Thebes, could not guard the many tombs located in the occupied region.

Stability returned once again in the New Kingdom, which began with the expulsion

The entrances to the tombs of Tutankhamun and Ramesses VI are visible near the center of this photo of the Valley of the Kings at sunset.

of the Hyksos. It seems certain that during this era, in which Egypt reached its zenith of power and had a strong central government, the royal tombs in the Valley of the Kings and other important burial sites were well guarded. That situation changed dramatically, however, when the New Kingdom gave way to the Third Intermediate Period (ca. 1069–747 B.C.). In this era Egypt once more suffered from weakness and divided government, and several surviving papyri record violations of tombs. These documents are mainly records of the trials and punishments of some of the thieves. One, the Amherst Papyrus, contains the confession of a tomb robber, which reads in part:

> The mummy of this king was all covered with gold, and his inner coffins were [covered with] gold and silver inside and outside, with inlays of all kinds of precious stones. We appropriated [took possession of] the gold which we found on this noble mummy . . . and on his eye amulets and his ornaments which were at his neck. . . . [We] found the royal wife . . . likewise and we appropriated all we found on her too. We set fire to their inner coffins. We stole their outfit [cache of personal items] which we found with

them, consisting of objects of gold, silver, and bronze, and divided them up among ourselves.[73]

To Understand Rather than Destroy

Some of the pharaohs whose tombs were looted in the Third Intermediate Period were among the greatest and most famous ancient Egypt produced. They included the renowned New Kingdom military conquerors Thutmose III and Ramesses II, as well as Thutmose I, Thutmose II, Seti I, and Ramesses III. In fact, so many royal and other upper-class tombs in the Valley of the Kings were pillaged that a group of concerned high priests and other local officials felt compelled to try to clean up the mess. They collected more than forty mummies of dead nobles, some of them damaged, and interred them together in one tomb at Deir el-Bahri on the west bank of the Nile, near Thebes.

Fortunately, thieves did not find this gravesite. And the bodies rested in peace until archaeologists discovered the tomb in 1881. This time those who disturbed the dead did not come to loot and destroy but, rather, to better understand and educate the world about the grand ancient Egyptian cultural and religious legacy.

Epilogue

THE LEGACY OF EGYPTIAN RELIGION

Though the ancient Egyptians are long since dead and their religion is no longer practiced, some of the individual beliefs, ideas, and symbols of that religion survive. Indeed, many aspects of the ancient Egyptian faith influenced other religions, including those of Persia, Greece, and Rome, as well as Christianity. Other aspects infiltrated and helped shape the art, architecture, and pop culture of the modern Western world.

Christian Images and Symbols

Among the most far-reaching of the surviving ancient Egyptian religious influences are those on Christianity. That faith, which was born in Palestine in the mid-first century A.D., began to take root in Egypt a few decades later and in the next few centuries slowly but surely spread across the land. Perhaps more than any other Mediterranean people, the Egyptians were quicker to iden-

tify with and embrace the concept of Jesus Christ as the son of God. As Richard Wilkinson points out, this was because "since ancient times [the Egyptians] had viewed their king as the incarnate son of a god."[74] So they had a strong traditional precedent for this concept.

After converting, early Egyptian Christians rejected many of the religious beliefs of their ancestors. As is only natural, however, they retained some, which subsequently helped to shape the emerging new faith. For example, consider the graphic ancient Egyptian depictions of those who failed to pass the judgment of Osiris. The endless torture and suffering of these souls in the nether world strongly influenced early Christian views of hell. Ancient images of Egyptian gods were also influential. In Egypt's Roman Period, some depictions of the iconic battle between Horus and Seth (in which Horus avenged the murder of his father, Osiris) showed Horus as a mounted Roman warrior, a sort of knight. This knight speared Seth, who appeared as a crocodile. Many scholars think that this was the basis for the many medieval artistic renderings and stories about St. George and the dragon.

Even more influential on emerging Christianity was the iconography associated with the goddess Isis. Both the Greeks and Romans adopted and worshipped Isis, emphasizing her roles as divine mother figure and bringer of religious salvation. The widespread artistic images of her cradling the baby Horus became the model on which early Christians based almost identical depictions of Mary holding the baby Jesus.

From Shopping Malls to Reincarnation

Many other influences of ancient Egyptian religion, some involving the dead, others more secular in nature, can be seen across the Western world. Pyramids are an obvious example. Numerous modern structures have adopted the pyramidal form in imitation of ancient Egyptian pyramid tombs. In Richmond, Virginia, a 90-foot-tall pyramid, erected in 1869, houses the bodies of 18,000 Confederate soldiers killed in the Civil War. In 1974 a 110-foot-tall copper-sheathed pyramid was built as a funeral home in Broward, Florida. Most famous of all is the Luxor Hotel in Las Vegas. Its mammoth Egyptianesque complex features not only a 350-foot-tall glass pyramid (larger than Menkaure's pyramid tomb at Giza) but also a huge replica of the great Giza sphinx; a museum with accurate replicas of the artifacts discovered by Howard Carter in King Tut's tomb; and a shopping mall dubbed the "Giza Galleria."

Pyramids are also thought by some people today to possess magical or healing powers. This stems in part from a widespread belief that the ancient Egyptians somehow possessed potent mystical abilities or knowledge that

A carving on the base of an ancient throne shows Horus fighting Seth.

The Luxor Hotel in Las Vegas is a glass replica of an ancient Egyptian pyramid-tomb. Replicas of the Great Sphinx and an obelisk are also visible.

remains unavailable to most other peoples. As Bob Brier puts it:

> To the layperson, hieroglyphs seem indecipherable and mysterious, and this . . . makes it seem that the ancient Egyptians had access to hidden wisdom. For Occultists and New Agers, Egypt is the imagined repository of all lost knowledge—the advanced civilization that had medical cures for all your ills.[75]

This belief in the mystical powers of ancient Egyptian religion and its original practitioners extends into modern beliefs in reincarnation and past lives. "There are an amazing number of people walking around today," Brier writes, "who believe they were ancient Egyptians in a previous life."[76] Interestingly, the ancient Egyptians themselves did not believe in reincarnation. That is why they invested so much time and energy in preserving the body and otherwise ensuring that they would live for eternity in the Underworld. Nevertheless, at the same time that many people today misunderstand and pervert ancient Egyptian religion, the continuing cultural influence of various aspects of that faith cannot be overlooked. It remains a testament to the genius of what was undeniably one of history's greatest peoples.

Notes

Introduction: The World's Most Religious People?

1. Herodotus, *The Histories*, trans. Aubrey de Sélincourt. New York: Penguin, 1972, p. 143.
2. Lionel Casson, *Everyday Life in Ancient Egypt*. Baltimore: Johns Hopkins University Press, 2001, pp. 79–80.
3. David P. Silverman, "Divinity and Deities in Ancient Egypt," in Byron E. Shafer, ed., *Religion in Ancient Egypt*. Ithaca, NY: Cornell University Press, 1991, pp. 17–18.
4. Silverman, "Divinity and Deities," p. 18.
5. Leonard H. Lesko, "Ancient Egyptian Cosmogonies and Cosmology," in Shafer, *Religion in Ancient Egypt*, pp. 90–91.
6. Richard H. Wilkinson, *The Complete Gods and Goddesses of Ancient Egypt*. London: Thames and Hudson, 2003, p. 15.

Chapter 1: The Gods and Their Realm

7. Wilkinson, *Complete Gods and Goddesses*, p. 15.
8. Casson, *Everyday Life*, p. 84.
9. Wilkinson, *Complete Gods and Goddesses*, p. 35.
10. Quoted in David P. Silverman, ed., *Ancient Egypt*. New York: Oxford University Press, 1997, p. 115.
11. Silverman, *Ancient Egypt*, p. 115.
12. Apuleius, *The Golden Ass*, trans. P.G. Walsh. New York: Oxford University Press, 1995, pp. 219–20.
13. David P. Silverman, "Deities," in Donald B. Redford, ed., *The Ancient Gods Speak: A Guide to Egyptian Religion*. New York: Oxford University Press, 2002, p. 95.
14. Herodotus, *Histories*, p. 156.
15. Silverman, "Divinity and Deities," pp. 15, 18.

Chapter 2: Major Creation Myths

16. Quoted in Redford, *The Ancient Gods Speak*, p. 246.
17. Vincent A. Tobin, "Creation Myths," in Redford, *The Ancient Gods Speak*, p. 250.
18. Tobin, "Creation Myths," p. 251.
19. Quoted in Josephine Mayer and Tom Prideaux, eds., *Never to Die: The Egyptians in Their Own Words*. New York: Viking, 1938, p. 25.
20. Quoted in Mayer and Prideaux, *Never to Die*, p. 25.
21. Wilkinson, *Complete Gods and Goddesses*, p. 18.

22. Quoted in Redford, *The Ancient Gods Speak*, p. 249.
23. Genesis 1:3.
24. John 1:1.
25. Tobin, "Creation Myths," p. 249.
26. George Hart, *Egyptian Myths*. Austin: University of Texas Press, 1995, p. 21.
27. Quoted in W. van den Dungen, trans., "Amun, the Great God: Hidden, One and Millions," Society for Philosophy, Antwerp, 2002. http://maat.sofia topia.org/amun.htm.

Chapter 3:
Rituals to Honor the Gods

28. Wilkinson, *Complete Gods and Goddesses*, p. 43.
29. Herodotus, *Histories*, p. 143.
30. Stephen E. Thompson, "Cults, an Overview," in Redford, *The Ancient Gods Speak*, p. 65.
31. Herodotus, *Histories*, pp. 144–45.
32. Herodotus, *Histories*, p. 153.
33. Quoted in Wilkinson, *Complete Gods and Goddesses*, p. 50.
34. Silverman, *Ancient Egypt*, p. 148.

Chapter 4:
Magic Spells and Amulets

35. Quoted in A.G. McDowall, *Village Life in Ancient Egypt*. New York: Oxford University Press, 1999, pp. 118–19.
36. Bob Brier, *Ancient Egyptian Magic*. New York: HarperCollins, 2001, p. 11.
37. Brier, *Magic*, p. 50.
38. Quoted in McDowall, *Village Life*, pp. 116–17.
39. Quoted in Brier, *Magic*, p. 61.
40. Brier, *Magic*, pp. 146–47.
41. Quoted in Brier, *Magic*, p. 167.

Chapter 5:
Beliefs About the Afterlife

42. Bob Brier, "Egyptomania: What Accounts for Our Intoxication with Things Egyptian?" *Archaeology*, January/February 2004, p. 18.
43. Casson, *Everyday Life*, pp. 103–104.
44. A. Rosalie David, *Handbook to Life in Ancient Egypt*. New York: Facts On File, 1998, p. 140.
45. Quoted in Miriam Lichtheim, ed., *Ancient Egyptian Literature: A Book of Readings*. vol. 2. Berkeley and Los Angeles: University of California Press, 1975–1976, pp. 124–26.
46. Quoted in Lichtheim, ed., *Ancient Egyptian Literature*, vol. 2, p. 127.
47. J.V. Dijk, "Hell," in Redford, *The Ancient Gods Speak*, p. 163.
48. Wilkinson, *Complete Gods and Goddesses*, pp. 119–20.
49. Silverman, *Ancient Egypt*, p. 106.

Chapter 6:
Mummies and Embalming

50. David, *Handbook to Life in Ancient Egypt*, p. 159.
51. Herodotus, *Histories*, p. 160.
52. Herodotus, *Histories*, p. 160.
53. Herodotus, *Histories*, p. 160.

54. Brier, *Magic*, p. 76.
55. Herodotus, *Histories*, p. 160.
56. Herodotus, *Histories*, p. 161.
57. Herodotus, *Histories*, p. 161.
58. Quoted in Brier, *Magic*, pp. 77–78.
59. Herodotus, *Histories*, p. 155.
60. Herodotus, *Histories*, p. 155.

Chapter 7:
Rituals to Honor the Dead

61. Ann M. Roth, "Funerary Ritual," in Redford, *The Ancient Gods Speak*, pp. 152–53.
62. Silverman, *Ancient Egypt*, p. 159.
63. Brier, *Magic*, p. 169.
64. Quoted in McDowall, *Village Life*, p. 120.
65. Ian Shaw, "Funerary Texts," in Ian Shaw and Paul Nicholson, *The Dictionary of Ancient Egypt*. New York: Harry N. Abrams, 1995, pp. 105–106.
66. Quoted in McDowall, *Village Life*, p. 121.
67. Silverman, *Ancient Egypt*, p. 164.

Chapter 8:
Tombs and Grave Goods

68. David, *Handbook to Life in Ancient Egypt*, p. 173.
69. Quoted in Nicholas Reeves, *Ancient Egypt: The Great Discoveries*. New York: Thames and Hudson, 2000, p. 127.
70. Reeves, *Ancient Egypt*, p. 127.

Chapter 9: Tomb Robbers
Violate the Dead

71. Dieter Arnold, *Building in Egypt: Pharaonic Stone Masonry*. Oxford, England: Oxford University Press, 1991, p. 219.
72. Arnold, *Building in Egypt*, p. 220.
73. Quoted in T. Eric Peet, *The Great Tomb Robberies of the Twentieth Egyptian Dynasty*. Hildesheim, Germany: George Olms, 1977, pp. 48–49.

Epilogue: The Legacy
of Egyptian Religion

74. Wilkinson, *Complete Gods and Goddesses*, p. 242.
75. Brier, "Egyptomania," p. 19.
76. Brier, "Egyptomania," p. 19.

Chronology

B.C.

ca. 5500–3100

Years of Egypt's so-called Predynastic Period, during which the country is divided into many small city-states and eventually into two major kingdoms—Upper Egypt and Lower Egypt.

ca. 3100–2686

Years of the Early Dynastic Period, encompassing the reigns of the nine rulers of the First Dynasty and seven rulers of the Second Dynasty.

ca. 2686–2181

Years of the Old Kingdom (encompassing the rulers of the Third, Fourth, Fifth, and Sixth dynasties), during which most of Egypt's pyramids are built, including the largest ones at Giza (near modern Cairo).

ca. 2181–2055

Years of the First Intermediate Period, which witnessed much civil strife and a partial breakdown of central authority and law and order.

ca. 2055–1650

Years of the Middle Kingdom (encompassing the Eleventh, Twelfth, Thirteenth, and Fourteenth dynasties), in which the Egyptians begin expanding their territory by conquest and their wealth through trade.

ca. 1650–1550

Years of the Second Intermediate Period, also called the "Hyksos" period in reference to an Asiatic people of that name who invaded and occupied Egypt.

ca. 1550–1069

Years of the New Kingdom (encompassing the Eighteenth, Nineteenth, and Twentieth dynasties), in which a series of strong pharaohs create an Egyptian empire and erect numerous large temples, palaces, and forts.

ca. 1069–747

Years of the Third Intermediate Period, during which Egypt falls into steady military, political, and cultural decline.

ca. 747–332

Years of the Late Period, during most of which members of foreign-born dynasties rule Egypt.

323–30

Years of the Ptolemaic Period (or Egypt's Greek Period), during which Ptolemy and his descendants rule Egypt.

30 B.C.–A.D. 395

Years of the Roman Period, in which a series of Roman emperors control Egypt.

Glossary

akh: The ability of all the soul's parts to exist indefinitely in the Underworld.

akhu: Spirits of the dead.

amulet: An object thought to possess protective magical powers.

ankh: A written sign or an object (sometimes an amulet) shaped like a cross with a loop at the top, which symbolized "life."

archaeology: The study of past civilizations and their artifacts.

ba: A part of the soul that could leave the body and grave and go anywhere.

bau: A manifestation of a god that sometimes punished human wrongdoers.

benben: In Egyptian mythology, the primeval mound of creation and first dry land in the world; or a sacred stone representation of the mound.

bimorph (or **hybrid**): A half-animal, half-human form of a god.

canopic jar: A container that held the internal organs of a person who was embalmed; such jars were placed in the tomb with the mummy.

cosmology: A description of the structure of the cosmos.

cult: In ancient times, the collected beliefs, temples, rituals, sacred objects, and priests of a god or gods.

cult temple: A temple used primarily for standard worship of a god or gods.

Duat: In ancient Egyptian cosmology, the region lying beneath the earth.

dynasty: A line of rulers belonging to a single family.

Egyptology: The branch of archaeology dealing specifically with ancient Egypt.

heka: Magic; or a mystical force possessed by divine beings.

iconography: Depictions of someone or something in paintings, sculptures, and other visual arts.

incubation: The process in which a god was said to reveal the future through images or other communication during a dream.

inscriptions: Letters and words carved into stone or some other durable material.

ka: A part of the soul that was thought of as its life force and remained in the grave or tomb.

manifestation: An alternate form or guise of a god.

mastaba: A low, rectangular tomb made of mud bricks or stone.

mortuary temple: A temple built mainly to maintain a deceased pharaoh's spirit and ensure its continued connection to the gods.

natron: A mineral salt used by ancient embalmers to dry out bodies and better preserve them.

negative confession: A group of chants from the Book of the Dead, each denying the commission of a sin; supposedly a deceased person recited the confession to the god Osiris in hopes of entering the Underworld.

netcher: A god; also used to denote various spirits and demons.

oracle: A person or statue that was believed to be a medium able to channel communication between the gods and humans.

pantheon: A group of gods worshipped by a people or nation.

papyrus: A water plant from which the Egyptians and other ancients made a kind of parchment; or a book or other written document made of that parchment.

portcullis: A door that slides down from above an entranceway to block that opening; portcullises consisting of slabs of stone were often used to block the entrances to Egyptian burial chambers.

saw: "Watch"; a group of priests whose members served in a temple for part of each year, in rotation with other groups.

scarab: An amulet or other object shaped like a scarab beetle.

shawabti (or **shabti**): A small figurine representing a worker; it was thought that such objects placed in tombs would magically come to life and perform labor in the afterlife.

stele (plural, **stelae**): A stone or wooden marker, often inscribed with text, pictures, or both.

udjat: An amulet representing and shaped like the Eye of Horus, consisting of the reassembled pieces of the god's eye, which was shattered in a fight with another deity.

zoomorph: The animal form of a god.

For Further Reading

Books

Barbara Adams, *Egyptian Mummies.* Buckinghamshire, England: Shire, 1998. A very informative overview of ancient Egyptian embalming of humans and animals, with a reading level aimed at advanced young readers and up.

Lionel Casson, *Everyday Life in Ancient Egypt.* Baltimore: Johns Hopkins University Press, 2001. An excellent, fascinating examination of ancient Egyptian life by a great scholar. Includes two chapters on Egyptian religion. (The reading level is high school and general adult.)

Tim McNeese, *The Pyramids of Giza.* San Diego: Lucent, 1997. This well-written volume explains in considerable detail why and how the Egyptian pyramids were built, as well as who built them.

Anne Millard, *Mysteries of the Pyramids.* Brookfield, CT: Copper Beach, 1995. Aimed at basic readers, this book by a noted scholar is short but brightly illustrated and filled with interesting facts about the pyramids and ancient Egyptian life.

David Murdock, *Tutankhamun: The Life and Death of a Pharaoh.* London: Dorling Kindersley, 1998. A beautifully illustrated examination of an Egyptian ruler who died young and was later forgotten, only to become famous in modern times when scholars unearthed his tomb.

Don Nardo, *Egyptian Mythology.* Berkeley Heights, NJ: Enslow, 2001. Aimed at intermediate readers, this book retells some of the most famous Egyptian myths, including the story of Osiris's murder by Seth.

Kelly Trumble, *Cat Mummies.* Boston: Houghton Mifflin, 1999. An unusual and nicely illustrated volume that explains why cats were important in ancient Egyptian society and how these animals were mummified.

Web Sites

Ancient Egyptian Magic (www.bbc.co.uk/history/ancient/egyptians/magic_01.shtml). Sponsored by the prestigious BBC (British Broadcasting Corporation), this site offers an excellent brief overview of the subject.

Glossary of Egyptian Gods and Goddesses (www.rom.on.ca/egypt/case/about/gods.html). Part of a very informative series presented by the Royal Ontario Museum, this site provides a list of the major deities and general information on each.

Mummy Maker (www.bbc.co.uk/history/ ancient/egyptians/mummy_maker_game. shtml). Another useful site from the BBC, this is an interactive game that allows people to take part in the simulated mummification of an Egyptian government official.

Pyramids: The Inside Story (www.pbs. org/wgbh/nova/pyramid). A very informational and entertaining resource sponsored by the prestigious television science program *Nova;* includes information on Egyptologist Mark Lehner and his groundbreaking studies and experiments related to ancient Egyptian construction.

Works Consulted

Major Works

Dieter Arnold, *Building in Egypt: Pharaonic Stone Masonry.* Oxford, England: Oxford University Press, 1991. A scholarly overview of Egyptian building methods, including a lengthy discussion of tombs and security measures designed to thwart tomb robbers.

Bob Brier, *Ancient Egyptian Magic.* New York: HarperCollins, 2001. An excellent summary of the subject, including clear explanations and examples of spells, amulets, curses, dreams, *shawabtis*, and so on.

———, *Egyptian Mummies: Unraveling the Secrets of an Ancient Art.* New York: William Morrow, 1994. One of the best available sources about mummies, including embalming techniques, beliefs about mummies, animal mummies, and modern movie versions of mummies.

A. Rosalie David, *Religion and Magic in Ancient Egypt.* New York: Penguin, 2002. A very informative and readable examination of religion through periods of ancient Egypt, supported by many primary sources and archaeological finds.

I.E.S. Edwards, *The Pyramids of Egypt.* New York: Penguin, 1993. One of the classic works about the pyramids, by one of the leading Egyptologists of the twentieth century.

George Hart, *Egyptian Myths.* Austin: University of Texas Press, 1995. A well-written, concise introduction to the subject.

Donald B. Redford, ed., *The Ancient Gods Speak: A Guide to Egyptian Religion.* New York: Oxford University Press, 2002. The most comprehensive single source of data about Egyptian religion, with nearly a hundred articles by a bevy of reliable Egyptologists and other scholars.

Serge Sauneron, *The Priests of Ancient Egypt.* Trans. David Lorton. Ithaca, NY: Cornell University Press, 2000. An informative, well-written study of Egyptian priests, with a lot of data on tombs and temples.

Byron E. Shafer, ed., *Religion in Ancient Egypt.* Ithaca, NY: Cornell University Press, 1991. A collection of a few long essays about Egyptian religious beliefs and rituals by noted scholars. Will appeal mainly to scholars and devoted buffs of the subject.

David P. Silverman, ed., *Ancient Egypt.* New York: Oxford University Press, 1997. A very useful general depiction of ancient Egyptian culture, with a large section on religion.

Steven Snape, *Egyptian Temples.* Buckinghamshire, England: Shire, 1999. Well illustrated, this is a good general introduction that discusses cult temples, mortuary temples, and atypical temples like those at Abu Simbel.

Richard H. Wilkinson, *The Complete Gods and Goddesses of Ancient Egypt*. London: Thames and Hudson, 2003. A highly comprehensive and useful guide to the Egyptian divinities and the symbols and rituals associated with them.

————, *The Complete Temples of Ancient Egypt*. London: Thames and Hudson, 2000. Similar to Snape's book (see above), but more comprehensive and more detailed.

Other Important Works

Primary Sources

Apuleius, *The Golden Ass*. Trans. P.G. Walsh. New York: Oxford University Press, 1995.

J.H. Breasted, ed., *Ancient Records of Egypt*. 5 vols. New York: Russell and Russell, 1962.

Herodotus, *The Histories*. Trans. Aubrey de Sélincourt. New York: Penguin, 1972.

Miriam Lichtheim, ed., *Ancient Egyptian Literature: A Book of Readings*. 2 vols. Berkeley and Los Angeles: University of California Press, 1975–1976.

Josephine Mayer and Tom Prideaux, eds., *Never to Die: The Egyptians in Their Own Words*. New York: Viking, 1938.

Pliny the Elder, *Natural History*, excerpted in *Natural History: A Selection*. Trans. John F. Healy. New York: Penguin, 1991.

Plutarch, *Isis and Osiris*, in *Moralia*. 14 vols. Trans. F.C. Babbitt. Cambridge, MA: Harvard University Press, 1936.

James B. Pritchard, ed., *Ancient Near Eastern Texts Relating to the Old Testament*. Princeton, NJ: Princeton University Press, 1969.

W.K. Simpson, ed., *The Literature of Ancient Egypt: An Anthology of Stories, Instructions, and Poetry*. New Haven, CT: Yale University Press, 1973.

Modern Works

Books

Paul G. Bahn, ed., *The Cambridge Illustrated History of Archaeology*. New York: Cambridge University Press, 1996.

Lionel Casson, *Ancient Egypt*. New York: Random House, 1983.

A. Rosalie David, *Handbook to Life in Ancient Egypt*. New York: Facts On File, 1998.

Sergio Donadoni, ed., *The Egyptians*. Trans. Robert Bianchi et al. Chicago: University of Chicago Press, 1990.

Nicolas Grimal, *A History of Ancient Egypt*. Trans. Ian Shaw. Oxford, England: Blackwell, 1992.

Zahi A. Hawass, *The Mysteries of Abu Simbel: Ramesses II and the Temples of the Rising Sun*. Cairo: American University in Cairo Press, 2001.

Mark Lehner, *The Complete Pyramids*. London: Thames and Hudson, 1997.

A.G. McDowall, *Village Life in Ancient Egypt*. New York: Oxford University Press, 1999.

T. Eric Peet, *The Great Tomb Robberies of the Twentieth Egyptian Dynasty*. Hildesheim, Germany: George Olms, 1977.

Stephen Quirke, *The Cult of Ra: Sun-Worship in Ancient Egypt.* London: Thames and Hudson, 2001.

Nicholas Reeves, *Ancient Egypt: The Great Discoveries.* New York: Thames and Hudson, 2000.

Nicholas Reeves and Richard H. Wilkinson, *The Complete Valley of the Kings.* London: Thames and Hudson, 1996.

George Reisner, *The Development of the Egyptian Tomb Down to the Accession of Cheops.* Brockton, MA: Pye Rare, 1996.

Ian Shaw and Paul Nicholson, *The Dictionary of Ancient Egypt.* New York: Harry N. Abrams, 1995.

Lewis Spence, *Ancient Egyptian Myths and Legends.* New York: Dover, 1990.

Eugen Strouhal, *Life of the Ancient Egyptians.* Norman: University of Oklahoma Press, 1992.

Angela P. Thomas, *Egyptian Gods and Myths.* Buckinghamshire, England: Shire, 2001.

Philip J. Watson, *Pyramids and Mastaba Tombs of the Old and Middle Kingdoms.* Princes Risborough, England: Shire, 1987.

Periodicals

Bob Brier, "Egyptomania: What Accounts for Our Intoxication with Things Egyptian?" *Archaeology*, January/February 2004.

E.L. Wilson, *Century Magazine*, vol. 34, May 1887.

Index

Aaron (Jewish prophet), 42
afterlife, 9, 49–57
    see also Underworld
Aha (pharaoh), tomb of, 76–77
Ahmose (pharaoh), tomb of, 78
akh (part of the soul), 51, 52
akhu (ghosts), 10
Amaunet (goddess), 27
Amenemhat II (pharaoh), 87
Amenhotep III (pharaoh), 73, 79
amulets, 45–46, 48
Amun (god), 11, 12, 15–16, 23, 27, 28, 70
    see also Amun-Ra
Amun-Ra (god), 10, 11, 15, 28, 37
Ancient Egyptian Literature (Lichtheim), 51, 55
animals
    gods' appearance as, 12
    mummification of, 63–65
    reverence for, 8, 18
    sacrifice of, 32, 34
ankh, symbol of, 46, 48
Anubis (god), 54
Apuleius (Roman writer), 16, 36
archaeologists, 79–80, 92
architects, 77–78, 84–85
Arnold, Dieter, 84, 90
art
    embalming process in, 61
    festivals in, 37
    Horus and, 17
    Osiris and, 16
    pharaohs and, 29
    representation of cosmos, 15
    Underworld in, 55
atef (crown), 16
Athena (Greek goddess), 37
Atum (god), 15–16, 23, 25, 26, 28
Atum-Ra (god), 25, 27

ba (part of the soul), 51, 52, 55
Bastet (goddess), 46, 64
Bat (goddess), 18
bau (messengers), 10

belief, in gods, 30
benben (sacred stone), 25, 28
    see also mound, primeval
Bent Pyramid, 88
Bible, 26, 42
bimorphs, 12
boats, 15, 69–70
bodies, preservation of, 49, 58–65
Book of the Dead, 53–54, 72
brain, embalming and, 61
Brier, Bob
    on ankh symbol, 48
    on embalming, 61
    on immortality, 49
    on magic, 41, 42
    on prayers, 60
    on scarab amulets, 46
    on shawabtis, 71
British Museum, 26
Brugsch, Emile, 86
Bubastis (city), 64
burial chambers, 88–90
Burton, James, 80

canopic jars, 61
Carter, Howard, 73, 80
Casson, Lionel, 7, 11, 49–50
cats, 64
cattle, reverence for, 8, 18
charity, 54
children, 46, 48, 83
Christianity, 10, 24–25, 30, 51, 93–94
clay, creation myths and, 28–29
cleanliness, priests and, 32
clergy. See priests
coffins, 60, 72
coffin texts, 72
Complete Gods and Goddesses of Ancient Egypt,
    The (Wilkinson), 13
cones, funeral, 70–71
cosmos, divine, 12–15
costs
    of embalming, 59–60

of funerals, 67
of pyramids, 78
of tomb guards, 90
craftsmen, god of, 25–26
creation myths, 9, 22–29
crocodile gods, 20–21
crocodiles, 8
crops, 16
crown, royal, 29
cult temples, 33

David, A. Rosalie, 51, 58, 65, 77
death. *See* afterlife
Deir el-Bahri, tomb at, 86, 92
demons, 10, 45
Dendera, temple at, 45
Dijk, J.V., 54
Diodorus Siculus (Greek historian), 61, 64
Djoser (pharaoh), tomb of, 77–78
Dream Book, 38
dreams, 38
drying agents, 62
dual gods, 11–12, 26
Duat, 14–15, 56

earthquakes, 15
Egypt, unification of, 9
Egyptian Mummies (Brier), 60
embalming process
    animals and, 63–65
    development of, 58–59
    drying and wrapping, 61–63
    embalmers and, 59–61
    removing internal organs, 61
employment, of priests, 31–32
Ennead, 25, 26, 28
Esna (city), 28–29
Evershed, Richard, 65
evil spirits, 66, 71
exorcism, 71
Eye of Horus, 46

falcons, 18
festivals, 30, 35–37
    see also specific festivals
"Field of Rushes," 55
First Dynasty, 84
First Intermediate Period, 91
funeral rites, 59, 66–74
see also embalming process

funerary cults, 69
funerary texts, 71–72

games, funerary, 66, 72–74
Geb (god), 15, 25
geography, creation myths and, 23
George, Saint, 94
ghosts, 10, 71
Giza, pyramids at, 78, 85, 91
God, Judeo-Christian, 26–27
gods
    afterlife and, 49
    amulets, 46
    animals and, 8
    artistic representations of, 29
    belief in, 30
    categories of, 10–12
    communication with, 37–38, 39
    homes of, 12–15
    human-like characteristics of, 21
    local, 9, 11
    minor, 17–21
    sacred images of, 32, 33–34
Golden Ass, The (Apuleius), 16, 36
Gospels, Christian, 24–25, 26
grave goods, 76, 80, 81–83
grave robbers
    political instability and, 90–92
    punishments for, 84, 92
    pyramids and, 78–79
    security measures against, 85–90
    Valley of the Kings and, 80, 83
graves, 58, 75, 76
    see also tombs
Greeks, Egyptian influence on, 6, 17
guards, for tombs, 90

Harem Conspiracy, 44
harmony, cosmic, 38–39
Harpocrates (Greek god), 17
Hart, George, 27
Hathor (goddess), 8, 18, 31, 40
Hauhet (goddess), 27
Hawass, Zahi, 76
health, 45, 48
heart
    embalming and, 61
    weighing of, 54
heaven, 51, 55–56
heka (magic). *See* magic

Heliopolis, 25
hell, 54–55, 93
Hermopolis, creation myths of, 27–28
Herodotus (Greek historian)
    on animals, 20, 34, 64
    on embalming, 61, 62
    on funeral rites, 59–60
    on Neith, 37
    on piety, 6, 9
    on priests, 32
Hey (god), 27
hieroglyphs, 95
holy water, 45
Homer (Greek poet), 72
Horus (god), 16, 17, 46, 57, 73–74, 93–94
household goddesses, 20
House of Life, 41–42, 44
humans, creation of, 22, 25, 28–29
human shape, gods' appearance in, 12
Huni (pharaoh), tomb of, 78
hunting, 82
Hyksos, 91–92
hymns, 28

Illiad, The (Homer), 72
images
    in magic, 43
    sacred, 32, 33–34, 38
    in tombs, 82–83
Imhotep (architect), 77–78
immortality, 49–51
incubation, 38
inheritance, of positions, 32
Intef II (pharaoh), 37
Isis (goddess), 16–17, 25, 36, 40–41, 57, 94
Islam, 10, 30, 51
Isle of Flame, 27–28
Iunu (city). See Heliopolis

Judaism, 10, 30
judgment of the dead, 53–54, 55

ka (life force), 51–52
Kauket (goddess), 27
Kek (god), 27
Kha (architect), tomb of, 75–76, 79–80, 81
Khafre (pharaoh), 78
Khemnu (city). See Hermopolis
Khepri (god). See Atum-Ra
Kheruef (steward), 73

Khnum (god), 12, 28–29
Khnum-Ra (god), 12
Khonsu (god), 37
Khufu (pharaoh), 78, 86–87, 88
kings. See pharaohs

lamps, 37
Launching of Isis's Ship, Festival of, 36
Lehner, Mark, 76
Leiden Papyrus, 28
Lesko, Leonard H., 9
Lichtheim, Miriam, 51, 55
linen, mummification and, 62
lions, 8
literature. See writing
Luxor Hotel, 94

magic, 40–48, 94–95
magicians, 41–43
marriage, goddess of, 20
masks, 82, 83
mastaba (tomb), 76–77, 84
McDowall, A.G., 20, 39
Mehet-Weret (goddess), 18
Mehun (god), 10
Memphis (city), creation myths of, 25–27
Menes (pharaoh), 9, 29
Menkaure (pharaoh), 78
Meryet (wife of Kha), 81
Middle Kingdom
    creation myths and, 28
    funeral rites, 67, 70
    immortality and, 50
    tombs, 85–86, 87, 91
Min (god), 12
Min-Amun (god), 12
monotheism, 10
Montet, Pierre, 80
Montu (god), 18
mortuary temples, 33
Moses, 42
mound, primeval, 25, 26, 27, 29
mummies, at Deir el-Bahri, 86
mummification. See embalming process
music, 82
Mut (goddess), 37

name, of the soul, 51, 52–53
natron (drying agent), 62
natural world, religion and, 7–8

Naunet (goddess), 26, 27
"negative confession," 51, 54, 72
Neith (goddess), 37
Nephthys (goddess), 25
netcher. See gods
New Kingdom
    funeral rites, 67, 69, 70, 71
    Thebes and, 28
    tombs, 79, 91–92
New Year Festival, 36
Nile River, 7, 14, 36, 70
Nile Valley, 22–23
Nun (god), 25, 26, 27
Nut (goddess), 15, 25

offerings, 30, 32, 34–35
Ogdoad, the, 27, 28
Old Kingdom
    afterlife and, 57
    funeral rites, 67
    immortality and, 49
    tombs, 85–86, 91
Olympic Games, 74
Opet, Festival of, 37, 69–70
oracles, 38, 39
organs, removal of, 60, 61
Osiris (god)
    afterlife and, 51, 56–57
    creation of, 25
    funeral of, 59
    judgment of the dead and, 53–54, 72
    murder of, 36
    role of, 10, 16

papyrus amulets, 46, 48
passageways, in tombs, 88
"Passing Through the Underworld" (game), 74
Pelasgians, 6
petitions, to the gods, 39
pharaohs
    afterlife and, 49, 57
    creation myths and, 24, 28
    games and, 74
    as gods, 7, 10, 17
    magic and, 44
    priests and, 32
phyles (gangs), 31–32
physical forms, of gods, 12
physicians, 45
political instability, 90–92

politics, religion and, 7, 29
Porphyry (Greek philosopher), 60
portcullises, 86–87
prayers, 30, 37, 60, 62–63
Predynastic Period
    immortality and, 49
    local gods and, 23
    natural world and, 8
priests, 7, 31–32, 41–42, 60
processions, funeral, 66–67
protection, magic for, 45–46
Ptah (god), 15–16, 23, 25–26, 28, 65
Ptolemaic Dynasty, 74
punishments, 64, 84, 92
pyramids, 75, 78–79, 85–90, 94–95
Pyramid Texts, 22, 25, 72

Ra (god)
    afterlife and, 55–56, 57
    Amun and, 11
    creation of, 27
    funeral rites and, 69, 70–71
    Hathor and, 31
    myths of, 40–41
    prayers to, 37
    role of, 15
Ra-Horakhty (god), 15
rain, 15
Ramesses II (pharaoh), 80, 92
Ramesses III (pharaoh), 44, 92
Ramesses IV (pharaoh), 15
Ramesses VI (pharaoh), 83
Re (god). See Ra
reincarnation, 95
religion
    ancient, 6
    differences with modern, 42, 50–51
    influence of Egyptian, 93–95
    natural world and, 7–8
    politics and, 29
resurrection, of Osiris, 57
rituals
    funeral rites, 66–74
    importance of, 30–31, 38–39
    magic, 43
Roth, Ann M., 67, 69

sacrifices. *See* offerings
salvation, 56–57
sand, burials and, 58, 89–90

saw (watches), 31
scarab amulets, 46
Schiaparelli, Ernesto, 79, 80
Second Intermediate Period, 91
security measures, for tombs, 85–90
Seeking and Finding, Festival of, 36
self-importance, Egyptian sense of, 23
Setau (worker), 71
Seth (god), 25, 36, 57, 73–74, 93–94
Seti I (pharaoh), 92
Shabaka Stone, 26
shadow, of the soul, 51, 53
Shafer, Byron E., 42
Shaw, Ian, 72
shawabtis (worker statues), 71, 72, 73
Shu (god), 15, 25
Silverman, David
    on cosmos, 15
    on development of religion, 8
    on funerary boats, 69–70
    on funerary games, 73
    on gods, 21
    on kingship, 57
    on rituals, 39
Sirius, 36
Sneferu (pharaoh), tomb of, 78, 88
Sobek (god), 20
social status, of embalmers, 60–61
Sokar (god), 18
Sopdu (god), 18
souls, 51–53, 58
speech, creation by, 26
spells, 43–44, 45
sphinx, 94
statues, of gods, 30
Step Pyramid, 78
sun, Ra and, 15
symbols, 46

Tanis, tombs at, 80
Ta-Weret (goddess), 20
Tefnut (goddess), 25
temples, 11, 32–34, 45, 60
Thebes (city), 28, 37
Third Intermediate Period, 92
Thompson, Stephen E., 34
Thoth (god), 13, 46, 54
Thutmose I (pharaoh), 92

Thutmose II (pharaoh), 92
Thutmose III (pharaoh), 92
Tiy (queen), 73
Tobin, Vincent A., 24, 25, 26
tombs
    mastabas, 76–78
    mummification and, 58
    pyramids, 78–79
    restored, 83
    security measures for, 85–90
    types of, 75–76
    Valley of the Kings and, 79–80
tools, 63, 82
Tutankhamun (pharaoh), 48, 73, 80, 81–82
Twenty-first Dynasty, 61
Twenty-sixth Dynasty, 90

udjat (amulet), 46
Unas (pharaoh), 72
Underworld, 13, 16, 49, 55–56, 57

Valley of the Kings, 79, 83
Village Life in Ancient Egypt (McDowall), 20, 39
votive offerings, 35

water, in Egyptian cosmology, 14
wealth, immortality and, 49–50
weapon, magic as, 43–44
Weeks, Kent R., 80
Wilkinson, Richard H.
    on Christianity, 93
    on development of religion, 9
    on gods, 11–12, 13, 25–26, 57
    on *netcher*, 10
    on rituals, 30–31
workers, on tombs, 88, 89
worship, 8–9, 33
wrapping, of bodies, 62
writing
    amulets and, 48
    funerary texts, 66, 71–72
    invention of, 13
    magic and, 41–42, 43
    offerings of, 35
    Pyramid Texts, 22, 25, 72
    religious, 30, 53–54

zoomorphs, 12, 18, 20–21

Picture Credits

Akg-images, 36, 38, 43, 62
Akg-Images/Werner Forman, 82(bottom)
© Aladin Abdel Naby/Reuters/CORBIS, 59
© Archivo Iconografico, S.A./CORBIS, 14, 50
Art Archive/Dagli Orti, 17, 41, 76, 89
The Art Archive / Egyptian Museum Turin / Dagli Orti, 82(top)
Art Archive/Musée du Louvre Paris / Dagli Orti, 63
Art Renewal.org, 67, 70
Art Resource, N.Y., 64
Bridgeman Art Library, 20
© Bettmann/CORBIS, 68
Borromeo/Art Resource, N.Y., 31, 32

© BSPI/CORBIS, 95
© Carmen Redondo/CORBIS, 33, 77
© Christine Osborne/CORBIS, 19
Erich Lessing/Art Resource, N.Y. , 12, 13, 47, 48, 73
© Free Agents Limited/CORBIS, 79
© Gianni Berto Vanni/CORBIS, 35
© Gianni Dagli Orti/CORBIS, 11, 18, 44, 53, 85, 94
© Michael Nicholson/CORBIS, 29
© Roger Wood/CORBIS, 91
© Ron Watts/CORBIS, 86
© Royalty Free/CORBIS, 81, 83
© Sandro Vannini/CORBIS, 7, 54
Steve Zmina, 26-27
Werner Forman/Art Resource, N.Y., 24, 56

About the Author

Historian and award-winning writer Don Nardo has written or edited numerous books about the ancient world, including *Empires of Mesopotamia*, *The Ancient Greeks*, *Life of a Roman Gladiator*, *The Etruscans*, *Ancient Civilizations*, and the *Greenhaven Encyclopedia of Greek and Roman Mythology*. Mr. Nardo lives with his wife, Christine, in Massachusetts.